RAILWAYS IN FOCUS

Ed Bartholomew & Michael Blakemore

NRM

NATIONAL
RAILWAY
MUSEUM

A newly-completed Great Northern Railway C1 class 4-4-2
locomotive with a rake of East Coast Joint Stock carriages at Bawtry
in June 1900. The train is on the 'wrong line' and although in steam it
is static, posed for the official photographers on the embankment. On
the right two photographers are using a large format glass plate
camera to take detailed views of the carriages. This perspective view
was taken on an 8½ × 6½ins wholeplate.

DON 387

RAILWAYS IN FOCUS

Ed Bartholomew & Michael Blakemore

Photographs from the National Railway Museum Collections

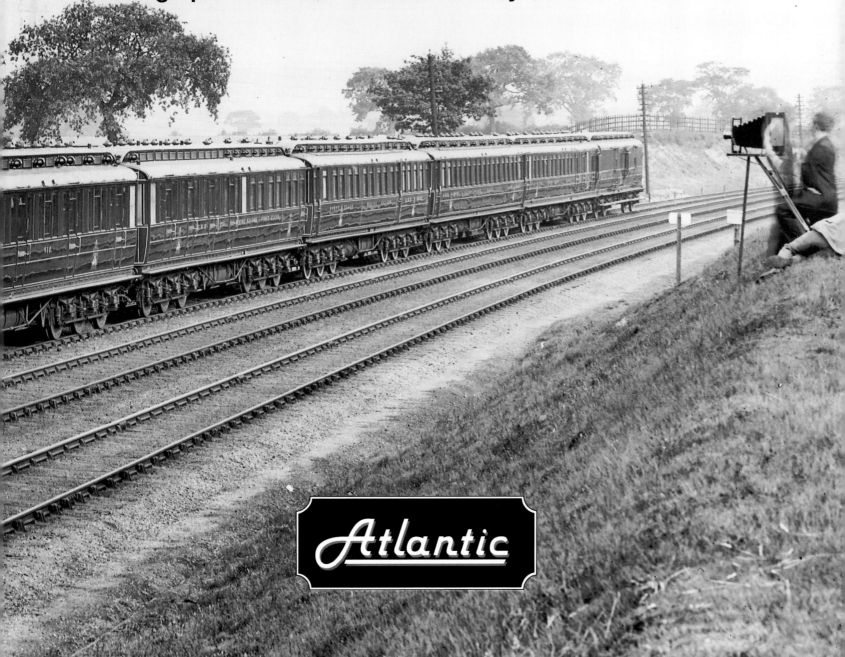

Atlantic

Published by Atlantic Transport Publishers, Trevithick House,
West End, Penryn, Cornwall, TR10 8HE

© Photographs, National Railway Museum 1998
© Text, National Railway Museum 1998

ISBN: 0 906899 91 5

Layout by Barry C. Lane, Sutton-in-Craven

Reproduction and printing by The Amadeus Press Ltd,
Huddersfield, West Yorkshire

British Cataloguing in Publication Data
A catalogue record for this book is available from the
British Library

CONTENTS

Acknowledgements

The authors would like to thank their colleagues at the National Railway Museum who contributed to *Railways in Focus*. Particular thanks go to the Head of Museum, Andrew Scott, and to Dieter Hopkin and Christine Heap who provided many thoughtful insights and constructive criticisms of the text and captions. Amba Kumar read and commented on the text, and Phil Atkins proved an invaluable source of information on the photographers and their images. John Perkin and Dave Sample spent many hours in the darkroom producing prints from sometimes difficult original negatives, and the NRM photographers, Chris Hogg and Lynn Patrick, provided both their own images of contemporary railways and high quality copies of some of the historic photographs held in the Museum's archives.

John Edgington, John Minnis and Brian Stephenson gave information on both the photographers and the images they produced, and helped to identify some of the places featured, as did members of the Great Eastern Railway Society. R C Riley, who played a major part in ensuring that the collections of many enthusiasts were preserved by the National Railway Museum, supplied biographical information on many of the photographers. Brian Radford who performed a similar role with some of the official collections, provided details of the Derby Works photographers.

Finally, David Joy of Atlantic Transport Publishers was extremely patient in his dealings with the NRM curators, whilst Barry Lane was responsible for the book's design and layout.

Needless to say, any errors and omissions are entirely the fault of the authors. The photographs included in this volume are all from the collections of the National Railway Museum, and prints may be made available for private study and research. Copies for reproduction purposes may be obtained from the Science & Society Picture Library at the Science Museum, London (Tel: 0171 938 9750).

BIBLIOGRAPHY

E Bartholomew & A Kumar	Guide To NRM Photographic Collections (NRM, 1997)
Maurice I Bray	Railway Picture Postcards (Moorland, 1986)
'L.C.'	Photography and the LMS, *LMS Magazine*, March 1938
Maxwell Craven (ed)	Keene's Derby (Breedon Books, 1993)
Maurice Earley	The Great Western Scene (Oxford Publishing Co, 1970)
Maurice Earley	My Best Railway Photographs (Ian Allan, 1946)
Colin Garratt	Great Railway Photographers, Maurice Earley (Milepost 92½, 1996)
Colin Garratt	Great Railway Photographers, E. R. Wethersett (Milepost 92½, 1996)
C C B Herbert	My Best Railway Photographs (Ian Allan, 1947)
C C B Herbert	More Of My Best Railway Photographs (Ian Allan, 1948)
Brian Morrison	The Steam Cameramen (Oxford Publishing Co, 1980)
Greg Norden	Landscapes Under The Luggage Rack (GNRP, 1997)
John Reed	Moving Images, Commemorating 40 Years of British Transport Films (Capital Transport, 1990)
T A Scotton	The Work Of A Railway Photographer, *LMS Railway Magazine*, July 1927
Jack Simmons	Image Of The Train: The Victorian Era (National Museum of Photography, Film and Television, 1993)
Jack Simmons	The Victorian Railway (Thames & Hudson, 1991)
Jack Simmons & Gordon Biddle (eds)	The Oxford Companion To British Railway History (Oxford University Press, 1997)
P Ransome-Wallis	My Best Railway Photographs (Ian Allan, 1948)
H Gordon Tidey	My Best Railway Photographs (Ian Allan, 1949)
H Gordon Tidey	Those Were The Trains (Ian Allan, 1957)
Eric Treacy	My Best Railway Photographs (Ian Allan, 1946)
Eric Treacy	More Of My Best Railway Photographs (Ian Allan, 1947)
Eric Treacy	Still More Of My Best Railway Photographs (Ian Allan, 1948)
V R Webster	'F Moore', The Story of A Notable Railway Artist, *Railway World* November 1984

FOREWORD

The National Railway Museum's photographic collections have formed an important source for researchers, writers and publishers for many years but this is the first time that a volume has been dedicated to the collection itself. This book aims to show readers the fascinating breadth of the collection and its quality and to illustrate just how the collection's images can illuminate the world of railway history.

The photographic collections have two main roles to play. Firstly, they are there to represent the best of the work of railway photographers, be they professionals working for the railway industry, specialist amateurs or outside observers of the railway scene. Secondly, the collection forms an important part of the body of information which the Museum holds and from which an understanding of the influence of the railway, its *modus operandi* and of the work of railway photographers can be gleaned.

Perhaps the most outstanding attribute of the collection is its breadth. The general expectation of a collection of railway photography might be that it is confined to images of trains; for since the invention of railways, the spectacle of the railway train as a powerful force in itself, or as a dynamic element in the landscape has fascinated each passing generation. The essential business of railways is to move people and things from A to B and emphasis should rightly be placed on the evidence of that movement. The Museum's photographic collections can produce such evidence in profusion, all of it technically proficient, some of it achieving the highest standards of creative photography. There is no doubt that the passing train is both spectacular and photogenic, and photographers of the calibre of Bishop Eric Treacy and Maurice Earley have captured the essence of the spectacle superbly well. But to move the trains around takes people, infrastructure, maintenance operations and a whole host of ancillary and support operations and it is in the photographic record of the activities that a whole new fascination reigns. As well as providing some compelling photography, this exploration of the NRM's collection provides ample evidence of the whole world that has been the railway. As the images chosen for inclusion here show, the spread of the railway's influence was tremendous and the photographic record held in the National Railway Museum's collections is similarly broad.

Despite those images of steam power in action, it is the people whose working and travelling lives are recorded which tend to produce the most memorable images. Some of the most stunning material in the collection is that relating to the construction of railways. Photographs from the earliest days of photography show navvies at work — or rather standing for the duration of the exposure — and were made not so very long after the pioneering records produced by the water colourist and illustrator J. C. Bourne. They open up a whole new window on a world previously only understood in sketchy outline. The majestic scale of the works of the railway age under construction contrast vividly with the mundane image of the rat catcher at work, yet the latter serves to remind us of the army of trades which were involved in running the railway. Images of railway road vehicles remind us of the influence of the railway on every corner of life. And the style of those photographs, recording the railway's service to an impossibly idyllic English village in the 1920s remind us that the role of the photographer as an image maker in the broadest sense of that term is nothing new.

As the manager of the National Railway Collection, one of the Museum's tasks is to build and care for a photographic collection to fulfil the roles I have already set out. Just as important is to place that collection before the public, whether researcher or general museum visitor. The tasks are huge. The Museum holds more than 1.5 million images on every conceivable medium from glass plate to CD-Rom. Access for users presupposes that there is for each image some form of reference information and a system to ensure that the images can be used without damage. Thanks to a dedicated team and the help of an increasing army of volunteer assistants, the proportion of the collection which is easily available to users has increased rapidly in recent years, in line with the Museum's commitment to bring all of its collections into the public arena. This volume is another aspect of that commitment, to ensure that as wide a public as possible can enjoy the wonderful material held in the collection and, in so doing, discover something more about the fascination of the world of the railway.

Andrew Scott
Head of National Railway Museum, 1998

INTRODUCTION

This book grew out of a longstanding project to celebrate the photographic collections of the National Railway Museum, and has provided a marvellous opportunity to demonstrate that railway photography has never been just about railways.

For over 150 years the camera has documented the development, decline and, in the recent past, the resurgence of the railways as they have shaped society. Official photographers have recorded the construction of new lines and vehicles, advertised their companies' services and depicted the daily lives of the railways' huge workforces of engineers, artisans, labourers and 'servants'. Enthusiasts meanwhile, fascinated by railway technology, have produced countless photographs of operating locomotives and passing trains. Whether professional or amateur, railway photographers have always proved keen to try new equipment and techniques and have consistently produced images of the highest quality.

We have selected images which are either striking photographs, or which enhance the story of railway photography. The photographs do not provide a chronology of the railways of Britain, nor a comprehensive coverage of every region. They do, however, provide a good cross section of the National Railway Museum's collections, so this eclectic grouping includes images which serve as records of vehicles, structures and the workplace, as advertisements, social documents, or as fine examples of creative photography.

Photographs in the Museum's collections are usually documented in the most simple terms and only rarely do the original registers and photographers' notebooks explain why they were taken. Of course, with notable exceptions, most railway photographs were never produced with the intention of their being reproduced in book form or displayed in museum galleries. Nevertheless, the passage of time confers significance on the most mundane photographs, and sometimes even basic record shots of damaged components can be appreciated for their aesthetic qualities.

Some railway photographers, for all their protestations that they were only making records of vehicles or buildings, clearly worked with an eye to posterity or the acclaim of their colleagues and were happy to submit their images for critical review. Typical were Eric Treacy or Maurice Earley, renowned for their views of magnificent locomotives in magnificent landscapes, or Cyril Herbert, who saw interesting shapes and forms in everyday structures. Even the official photographers, whose job it was to document the humdrum and commonplace, spoke the language of the creative photographer and applied their personal visions to everyday tasks.

Whatever the reasons they were taken, railway images nearly always convey the photographers' love of their subject, often echoing the work of more widely recognised practitioners. Through their idealized views of workers and passengers, imposing studies of grand buildings and speeding locomotives or drab urban landscapes beautified by the camera, generations of photographers have left us with an invaluable legacy by focussing on railways. The National Railway Museum continues to build on that legacy, regularly acquiring new images to add to the world's most important archive of railway photographs.

Ed Bartholomew
Michael Blakemore
York 1998

Part One

RAILWAYS AND PHOTOGRAPHY

'Panning' shots of locomotives at speed need a measure of skill and a steady pair of hands but the results can be quite dramatic. The impression of speed is particularly heightened in this case by the small 5ft driving wheels of British Railways 9F 2-10-0 No. 92204 which Tom Williams photographed on the Great Western main line south of Birmingham in September 1964. The 9Fs were designed for heavy freight haulage at moderate speeds but their use on passenger trains was not uncommon, especially in the busy summer period, and they could show a surprising turn of speed.

Williams 10057

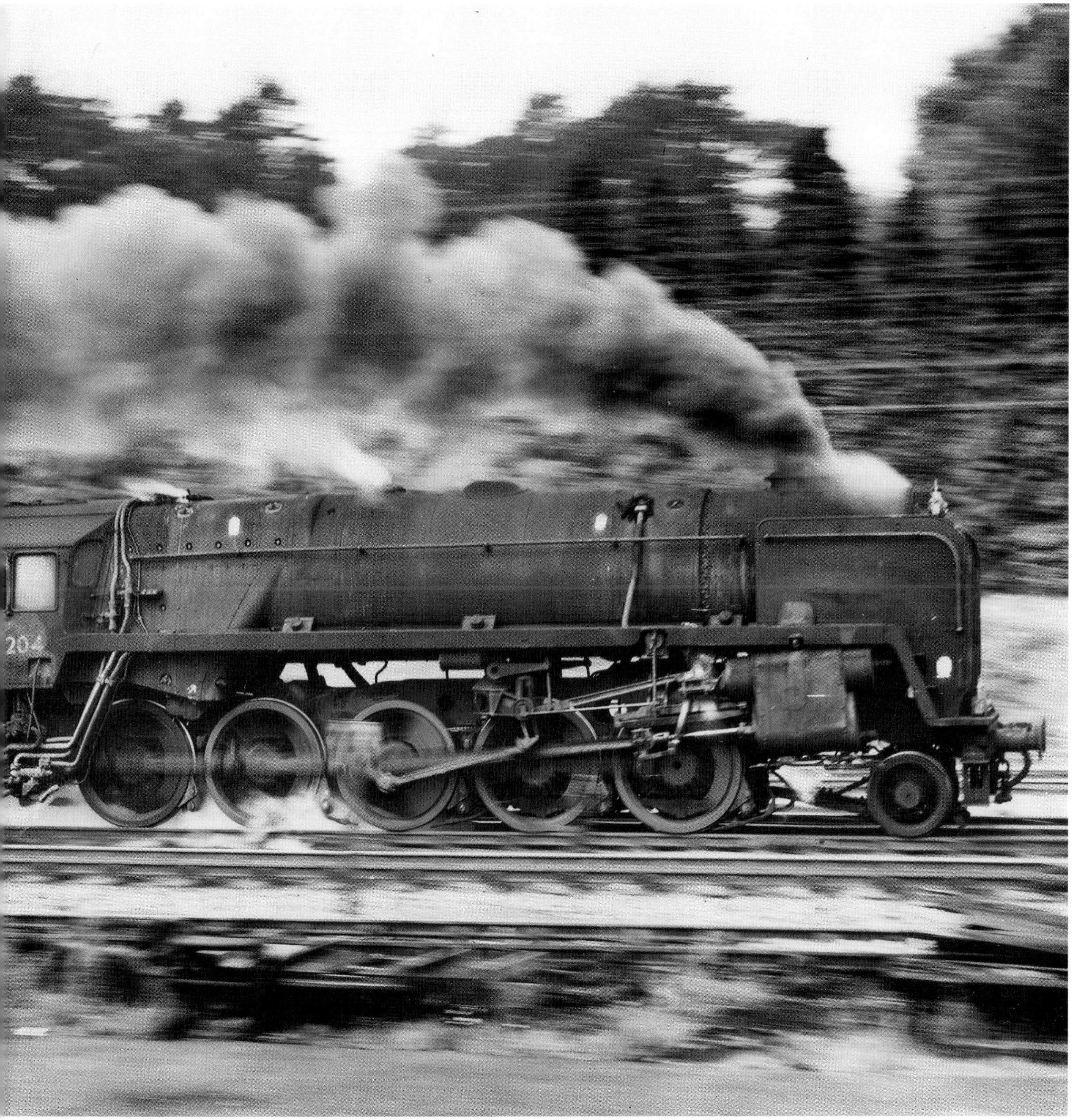
204

"Railways are in my blood"[1], declared Cyril Herbert when asked to explain his passion for railway photography, and his opinion has been echoed by countless others who have passed their days in stations, engine sheds and at the lineside, cameras at the ready. The camera and the railway have been closely linked since the earliest days of photography and within a few years of the invention of the first viable processes photographers had begun to depict railway subjects. The earliest known railway photograph was taken in 1845, when the Scottish artists David Octavius Hill and Robert Adamson produced a daguerreotype of Linlithgow, the foreground dominated by the town's newly-completed station on the Edinburgh & Glasgow Railway. In the same year Daniel Gooch, the youthful Locomotive Superintendent of the Great Western Railway, was photographed alongside a model of one of his designs, a 'Firefly' class locomotive. By 1847 I. K. Brunel was reported to be sending daguerreotype copies of his engineering drawings to prospective railway builders in Italy and Austria. In 1853 his competitor, Charles Blacker Vignoles, employed John Cooke Bourne and Roger Fenton to photograph the construction of his road bridge over the Dnieper. Vignoles was a founder member of the Photographic Society of London — later to become the Royal Photographic Society — and at its inaugural meeting that year lectured on ways in which engineers could make use of photography in their work.[2]

Contractors and railway companies followed Vignoles' advice and commissioned photographers to document their work and as Britain was criss-crossed by an ever expanding network of lines the camera was occasionally on hand to capture the latest inspiring projects. For many Victorians the railways epitomised progress, so it seemed fitting to them that the new medium was used to document the march of technological development. One of the earliest British engineering schemes to be photographed was the construction of the Britannia Bridge over the Menai Straits between 1847 and 1851 and during the course of the next decade the building of Brunel's Royal Albert Bridge across the Tamar and his suspension bridge over the Wye at Chepstow were both photographed.

In an empirical age the camera was viewed as the infallible recorder of objective truth and some engineers exploited this to good effect. In 1863 John Hawkshaw presented a Parliamentary committee with photographs which he claimed demonstrated the difficulties of building railway bridges to conform with exacting legal requirements. It took a while for photography to become standard practice amongst railway engineers and images of the early years of construction are comparatively rare, but by the 1860s the camera had become more commonplace on the building site. John Fowler, for example, employed James Flather and several other photographers to record the construction of London's Metropolitan

Railway, the world's first underground line. In 1867 the Midland Railway commissioned John Ward and J. B. Pyne to photograph the building of the London extension line to St. Pancras station, producing two magnificent volumes of albumen prints which include some of the earliest photographs of navvies at work. St. Pancras was also photographed for the Butterley Company, which provided the ironwork and kept images of the erection of the roof to show to potential customers. This practice was also adopted by John Bayliss, the contractor for the construction of the Midland Railway's Mansfield to Southwell line who, in 1872, produced several copies of an album of images which he told the Institution of Civil Engineers showed "that the most ordinary of our railway works may be treated artistically by photographers; and if so treated will present very pleasing and possibly instructive pictures".[3]

The invention of the collodion wet plate process in 1851 transformed photography, for it became possible to produce multiple copies of images, printed from sensitised glass plate negatives. Professional studios sprang up in almost every town, and many amateurs were encouraged to take up the camera. Like Vignoles and Hawkshaw, they used photography to document the world around them and were inevitably attracted to railway building, as new lines ripped through the landscape, founding new towns along their routes and bringing upheaval to the most remote rural communities. Local photographers, such as Richard Keene of Derby, recorded the changing scene through their images of a countryside scarred by embankments, cuttings and stark new viaducts and, in a rare image by an unknown photographer, raucous navvies celebrating a gala day at Bosworth.

There were, of course, photographers who were more interested in mechanics than civil engineering. They were lured to the railways by the raw power of the steam locomotive, but their attempts to produce dramatic images were often frustrated, because the early photographic emulsions were too slow to capture movement or the effects of clouds of smoke and steam. This subject was best treated by artists, most notably J. M. W. Turner, who in his 1844 painting 'Rain, Wind and Speed' showed what could be done "even with an ugly subject".[4] The first locomotive enthusiasts, however, saw beauty in this ugliness and concentrated their efforts on machinery rather than the railway landscape. Foremost amongst them was R. H. Bleasdale of Warwick, who began photographing locomotives in about 1857. Some of his first photographs were of the Stockton & Darlington Railway's original engines for, like countless railway enthusiasts who followed him, he was anxious to record historic lines and locomotives before they disappeared for ever. Bleasdale received considerable cooperation from the railway companies, who obligingly posed their different classes of locomotives in sidings or yards. He was also allowed special access to the railway factories and produced, for example, a series of thirty views of the Great Western Railway's Swindon Works which were mounted on cards and offered for sale in albums. Bleasdale travelled virtually the whole of Britain's railway network to photograph locomotives, using $8\frac{1}{2} \times 6\frac{1}{2}$ins wholeplates from which he produced albumen contact prints. He left a remarkable archive, for by his retirement in the early 1890s he had produced over 3,000 railway images.[5]

The railway companies, too, began to realise the benefits of photographing their newly-completed locomotives. The first to do so was the independent builder, Beyer, Peacock of Manchester. The company's founder, Charles Beyer, had himself experimented with daguerreotypes and in 1856 he persuaded a renowned local photographer, James Mudd, to produce images of locomotives and machinery which could be used by salesmen overseas to advertise the company's products. Initially Mudd employed Fox Talbot's waxed paper calotype negatives, but the resulting prints were not always a success, for Beyer showed the correspondent of *The Engineer* a photograph of a locomotive which he likened to "a cow in the dark".[6] Mudd soon adopted wet plate glass negatives, which gave better definition and were easier to handle than the flimsy and delicate calotypes.

Beyer, Peacock's example was shortly followed by the main railway operating companies. In the early 1860s the Midland Railway's John Warwick, a keen photographer who worked in the Signalling and Telegraph Department at Derby, photographed rolling stock and buildings as part of his duties. On gaining promotion he suggested that the company employed the services of his friend, Richard Keene, who owned a studio near the works. Keene, like Warwick an acquaintance of Fox Talbot, was an accomplished photographer who produced numerous images for the Midland Railway between about 1867 and 1873, but eventually found that his expanding business left him no time for railway work.[7] His role was largely taken over by Thomas Scotton, originally an amateur photographer who had been employed as a carriage painter in Derby Works but who also acted as Keene's assistant. As the Midland Railway's business expanded, photography played an increasingly important part in Scotton's work and thanks to the influence of Warwick and the Locomotive Superintendent, Samuel Johnson, in September 1882 he was appointed as the company's first official photographer on a salary of £1 12s (£1.60) per week. A year later Scotton was joined by his son, also called Thomas, who was paid 5s 8d (29p) a week to act as his father's assistant.[8]

In the last quarter of the nineteenth century all of the major railway companies employed official photographers. The first to establish its own unit was not the Midland, but the London & North Western Railway, which in the 1870s took on photographers at Crewe Works. By 1889 W. M. Acworth in his classic, *The Railways of England,* could acknowledge that the photographer was "a not unimportant official" in the company hierarchy, noting that "perhaps it is reported to the engineer that a viaduct shows signs of giving way, that a wall has cracked or an embankment slipped, and in the first instance, if the damage is only slight, instead of going himself to see the state of affairs, he sends the photographer to record it for him. Or, if an accident has happened, there can be no dispute afterwards how the engine was lying, or whether such-and-such a carriage left the metals, once a commission has been issued to take the evidence of the sun". Of course, photographers formed only a tiny fraction of the railways' huge workforce and although Acworth was aware of their significance he devoted as much space to the role of cats in the Midland's Trent sack store as the work of the Scottons at Derby![9]

An important element of the official photographer's work was producing images of newly-completed or refurbished locomotives and rolling stock, and this was carried out on such a regular basis that a standard procedure soon developed. It remained in place for decades. Locomotives selected for photography were usually painted in a special 'works grey' livery, a shade best suited for reproducing detail on glass plate negatives, for some colours, notably red, were not registered accurately by the photographic emulsions of the day. The engines were painted with the usual decorative linings in black and white, together with the company names and crests, then fitted with their nameplates and numbers. When the photographs had been taken they were returned to the shop and, no doubt to the frustration of the painters, the grey livery was covered in the standard company colours and the crests, lining and lettering applied once more. At Crewe, locomotives were photographed against a specially-constructed background of white sheeting, although at most other works the setting was more likely to be the paintshop or works wall. Vehicles were usually photographed from both sides, in perspective and from either end. Detailed shots were normally taken of any unusual or experimental features, but overhead views were rare, for no works had a specially-constructed gantry on which a heavy tripod and camera could be mounted.

The negatives were large, typically 15×12ins, and even, on occasion, 30×20ins. The large glass plates remained in use for many years, but during the latter part of the twentieth century were eventually superseded by $8\frac{1}{2} \times 6\frac{1}{2}$ins wholeplates and $6\frac{1}{2} \times 4\frac{3}{4}$ins quarterplates for all but the most prestigious jobs. To ensure fine definition the lens diaphragm was set at the smallest aperture, typically f45, which meant that exposures were long, often 50 or 60 seconds even in good weather.[10] Once the negatives had been processed they were varnished and any obtrusive features in the background removed, a chore usually performed by a team of photographic assistants. Pieces of card were stuck to the negatives to cover large, unwanted areas of sky or buildings and any remaining

The Fitting Shop in Crewe Works on 30th March 1906. The London & North Western Railway had introduced machine tools in the 1860s and 1870s in advance of many other industries and the workshops were, according to the company's Chief Mechanical Engineer, C. J. Bowen-Cooke, "a perfect maze of pulleys, straps, shafts and revolving wheels".

Crewe A 522

background carefully painted out with retouching ink. At Derby in the 1920s the negatives were mounted on easels or sloping desks while the assistants performed this tedious task, using drawing pens, sable brushes and curves to apply a mixture of Indian ink diluted with chromate of lead. The images which resulted were generally of the highest technical quality, with fine detail reproduced with superb resolution. At some works, therefore, glass negatives were still used in the 1970s to photograph newly-completed locomotives, although by this time the expense of the works grey paint scheme could no longer be justified.

The official photographers did not just apply themselves to completed vehicles, for they regularly ventured into the workshops to record construction and refurbishment, covering every stage in the production process from raw materials to the finished item. Taking photographs for use in exhibitions and brochures, but with an eye to posterity, they have left an extraordinary record of technological development in Britain. At the London & North Western Railway's Crewe Works, for example, innovative processes such as the Bessemer steel works, the introduction of machine tools or the use of a 2,000 ton steam hammer to forge axles were all photographed. At Horwich Works the Lancashire & Yorkshire Railway photographed each workshop in turn over a number of years and in doing so documented the changes in working patterns as, for instance, hydraulic riveters replaced the teams of fitters armed with sledgehammers who had previously assembled boilers.

Photography in the noisy, crowded and sometimes dingy workshops required considerable skill and the official photographers were clearly proud of their work. The Scottons, for instance, were both members of the Derby Photographic Society and frequently displayed their work in exhibitions and competitions. Shortly before his death in 1894 Thomas Scotton Senior showed off his images of locomotives, which the *British Journal of Photography* remarked were, "highly meritorious, as all this gentleman's works are, whilst T. Scotton's views of interiors of Midland Railway Buildings were admirable"[11]. The younger Thomas Scotton after starting out, like many official photographers, as an assistant, retired in 1932 after working for nearly fifty years in the Midland, later London, Midland & Scottish Railway, studio in Derby. Made a Life Fellow of the Royal Photographic Society, but aware of his own beginnings, he was enthusiastic in his support of amateur photographers. A Derby Railway Institute Photographic Society was founded in 1911 with the Chief Mechanical Engineer, Sir Henry Fowler, as its first President and the LMS later had its own society. Scotton evidently took his craft seriously, for in a 1925 article in the *LMS Railway Magazine* he informed the company's hobbyist photographers that "to succeed you have got to put your whole heart and soul into it".

For photographers such as Thomas Scotton, who believed that "to be able to see pictures, one must acquire the pictorial sense, and learn to know their structure and the reason of their beauty and charm", producing a seemingly endless stream of images of newly-completed vehicles or damaged components must have seemed rather mundane. The official photographer's role, however, soon began to extend way beyond the confines of the workshop and the studio and offered him far greater opportunity to exercise his skill.

In 1884 the Great Eastern Railway commissioned Payne Jennings, described by a company official as "the greatest landscape ·photographer of the time"[12], to produce scenic views of picturesque locations served by the railway. They were used to decorate carriages, in an attempt to encourage passengers to travel further afield on the company network. The original images were very simple, small views with handwritten captions, condemned by some cost-conscious GER managers as "a waste". However, the concept was soon taken up by other railway companies and Payne Jennings began producing similar views for the North Eastern and the London, Chatham & Dover Railways. The Midland Railway sent the Scottons out to take scenic views, but other companies employed the services of Payne Jennings, who by 1898 was publishing some 110,000 prints annually. The Great Western,

Lancashire & Yorkshire, London & South Western, South Eastern & Chatham, Midland, Great Central and Great Northern Railways preferred colour images in their carriages and these were supplied by the Photocrom Company. At its Tunbridge Wells factory Photocrom produced tinted photographs on an industrial scale and by 1900 employed eight photographers and had developed an archive of over 12,000 subjects. Photocrom images were even used to decorate a Royal Train, but they did not please everybody. Scott Damant, of the Great Eastern Railway, claimed that "viewed separately they are often not unpleasing, but a whole row of them is certainly not artistic. They all display the same blue sky, the same green trees and the same red roofs to the houses; consequently they are untrue to nature. Mr. Payne Jennings's monotones, on the other hand, are really artistic in every sense of the term. They cannot but effect a refining influence on all blessed with the slightest appreciation of the beautiful, and what is more, they are apt to prove an almost irresistible inducement to visit the spots they depict".[13]

Photocrom continued to maintain a large share of the market, but increasingly railway companies produced their scenic views in house, printed in· black and white or sepia tones. At Derby Works in the 1920s two adjacent darkrooms were set aside for enlarging, mainly for the production of carriage prints. A wholeplate camera with an arc lamp as its light source projected the image through a hole in a sliding shutter set into the wall onto 26 × 10ins bromide paper held in a groove on a table. Scotton and his assistants, undoubtedly to the horror of the purists, often double printed, for they liked to include clouds from other photographs to enliven drab skies. By 1926 the Derby photographers were supplying the LMS with about 5,000 carriage prints a year, but within a few years production had risen to an annual output of 15,000 to 20,000 sepia photographs.[14] The main drawback was that these images dated quickly, particularly as the more popular resorts regularly improved their facilities, so official photographers had to continually update their archives. In 1932, for instance, the LMS photographers based at Derby and Euston took 300 new negatives from which carriage prints could be produced. Eventually the LMS, like other railway companies, decided that it would be more economical to commission artists to produce the prints, for they could exercise licence by ignoring any feature which would date too quickly. Mr. Lambert of the Photocrom Co. objected that the skilled camera man was also an artist and that the public preferred illustrations of "places as they see them",[15] but by nationalisation in 1948 photographs had almost completely disappeared in favour of standard-sized colour prints.[16] Nevertheless, the more parsimonious railways still obliged their photographers to produce images for artists' reference, as it was considered more economical to send a man with a camera out into the country than to pay the expenses of an artist who spent several days at a site drawing from life!

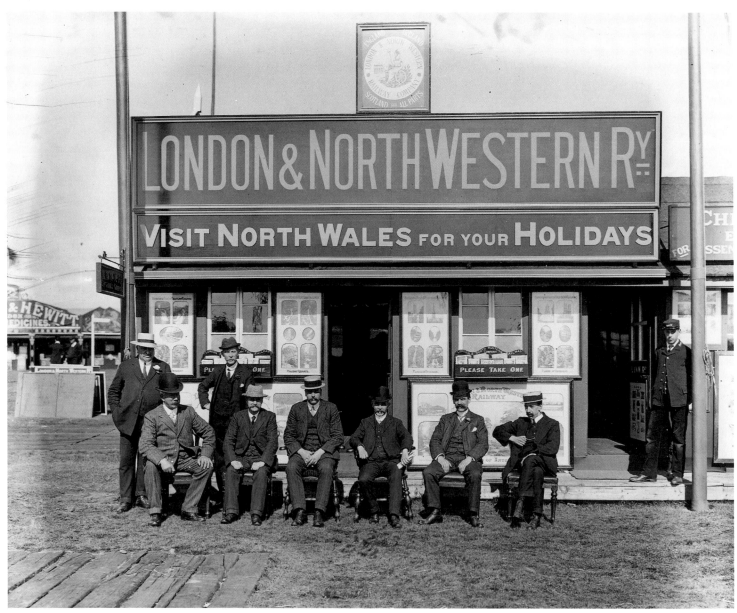

Crewe   MC 408

The publicity-conscious railways did not produce their most attractive photographs purely to decorate carriages. By the turn of the century company officials had realised that they could use photography in their advertising as an 'objective' record of their facilities and services, to complement the more abstract approach of the poster artists. Intended to appeal to an increasingly visually-literate public, photographs of vehicles and facilities began to appear on exhibition stands at fairs and shows. In a series of photographs taken at the Royal Lancashire Show in 1909, for instance, officials of the London & North Western Railway pose confidently in front of their enquiry office which advertises holidays in North Wales. On the walls behind are photographs of places of interest and one view of a train arriving at Llandrindod Wells station to show them how to get there (see above). On adjacent stands the Lancashire & Yorkshire, Furness, South Eastern & Chatham, Great Western, North Eastern, Great Northern, Great Central,

Great Eastern, Cambrian and Midland all prominently displayed photographs of places they served.

The Great Western Railway, however, was not content to rely on publicity stands alone and in 1904 commenced publication of an illustrated guide, *The Cornish Riviera Express*. It was followed in 1906 by *Holiday Haunts*, a brochure filled with official photographs of resorts and attractions in the company's operating area. It came to be published annually and in later editions also advertised the Channel Islands, Britanny, Isle of Man, the Scilly Isles, and Ireland, which could all be reached by GWR ferry services. With the exception of the war years *Holiday Haunts* appeared each March until the GWR was nationalised in 1948 and, sold at most for 6d (2½p), placed the work of the company photographers before an annual audience of some 200,000.[17]

In the years before the First World War official photographs found another publicity outlet in the form of postcards, col-

Two London & North Western Railway 2-4-2T locomotives haul a London-bound passenger train into Llandrindod Wells station in Wales, in about 1905. This official image was used in LNWR publicity and appears on the company stand at the Royal Agricultural Show at Southport in 1909, reproduced opposite (Crewe MC 408).

LMS 52

lected with such intensity that by 1914, when wartime paper shortages effectively ended the craze, the London & North Western Railway had printed over 11 million. The first railway postcard photograph appeared in Britain in 1894 and featured the Snowdon Mountain Railway, which ironically did not open to the public for another two years. 'Official' postcards were not issued for another four years, when the Great Eastern Railway used them to publicise its hotels and ships, but soon other companies were producing postcards which could be sold on station platforms by automatic vending machines.

Typical subjects were the standard works photographs of new locomotives in their grey liveries, company hotels and ferries, reproduced in printed form and as photogravures. Carriage interiors were popular, as were images of express trains at speed and on some lines passengers could write their messages during the journey and ask an attendant to post their cards at the next station. Some have doubted whether this branch of the official photographer's work was an effective form of advertising[18], but it certainly brought the railways' activities to public notice, encouraged a massive interest in locomotive design and performance, and probably inspired many enthusiasts to take up railway photography themselves.

An increasing awareness of the value of publicity widened the role of the official photographer and the railways began to establish specialist units at their London headquarters to supplement the departments based at their works. By the first years of the twentieth century the LNWR's photographers at Euston and the GWR's men at

The arrival of the railways in the Lake District stimulated tourism and visitors came in large numbers. With them came developments to meet their needs, including the promoters of tours, and in 1909 a charabanc is seen leaving the LNWR station at Windermere for the bumpy ride to Grasmere. An intriguing feature of the photograph is the ghostly figure of a boy standing to the right of the cyclist, partially removed from the glass plate with retouching ink.

LMS 1783

Paddington were already travelling the networks, producing views of pleasing countryside, towns and villages, images of speeding trains and a record of any innovation which reflected favourably on the companies' progressive philosophies. So, the Euston men were sent north to chronicle the 'motor' running between Windermere and Ambleside whilst the Paddington photographers provided images of their company's expresses on the approach to Bath. Publicity departments became increasingly sophisticated in the succeeding years, employing officials who had worked with newspapers and who understood the journalist's appetite for new stories, and the production of press photographs became an important part of the work of photographers like the GWR's Stan Micklewright. The canny Euston photographers contributed 'news' pictures of significant events, such as the images of *Coronation*'s record-breaking run between London and Crewe in June 1937, and 'features' photographs chosen for their pictorial impact.[19] Many official photographs were taken in the hope that a newspaper or magazine would use them as 'space fillers' and, in doing so, maintain the public profile of the railways. Style was important in these photographs. Genuine passengers were replaced by models, posed in the most luxurious carriages, and the negatives were sometimes manipulated, with pleasant countryside scenes positioned in the windows to replace the drab sidings at Swindon or Crewe which appeared on the originals. In the 1930s *the* style was streamlined and the LMS's numerous images of the sleek, bulbous-nosed 'Coronation' class locomotives were matched by the LNER's pictures of its A4 Pacifics, particularly the prestigious 'Silver Jubilee' and 'Coronation' services, which were introduced with fanfares and photography in the 1930s.

By the beginning of the twentieth century the works photographers' tasks had also increased. In addition to furnishing official records of all new types of locomotives, road vehicles

In 1936 the Great Western Railway photographed models posed in the compartment of a carriage, which was parked in a convenient siding, to advertise its 'Cornish Riviera' service from London to Penzance. The resulting print was altered through the addition of a scenic view of St. Michael's Mount in Cornwall placed over the window and then it was re-photographed. The evidence of this 'doctoring' can be seen at the window edges, along the curtains and around the man's head.

GWR B 12703

and rolling stock they undertook publicity work, covering naming ceremonies, the opening of new buildings and other official functions. The photographers' tasks brought some hazards. During the First World War the Midland's Thomas Scotton was arrested whilst photographing a munitions factory as part of his official duties and at Lancaster a crowd of workers threatened to throw him in a river as a spy.[20] In peacetime, photographers were expected to be on hand to record the aftermath of any major incidents and from an early date companies provided their staff with telephones at home so that they could be ready to respond at any time. The 'incidents' ranged from pilfered packing cases to serious collisions, or the gruesome evidence of suicides and accidents. Official photographers also provided 'mug shots' of thieves and fare dodgers and photographs of landslips, walls and fences for use by the legal departments in boundary disputes. The "evidence of the

sun" was no longer beyond question, however, for if official photographs were used as testimony in court cases or inquiries the photographers had to appear to prove that they were genuine. Photographs were also required as 'evidence' by the railways' specialist departments, particularly detailed metallurgical studies of broken axles, wheels and components, or microscopic images used in scientific research.[21]

A monotonous, but important, job was the reproduction of engineering drawings, which was initially performed using Herschel's ferroprussiate blueprint process. This was later replaced by 'Pellet' prints and then ferro-gallic papers. At first the copies were frame printed by exposure to daylight, but in the late 1890s electric copying became commonplace. This, in turn, was supplanted by the 'true-to-scale' dry process which, as its name suggests, ensured that any reproduction was exactly the same as the original, vital when one considers that a works photographic unit could provide as many as 44,500 tracings in a single year and it was essential that they were accurate.[22]

Although the official photographers were inventive in their use of publicity pictures and for many years led in the field of industrial photography, in technical matters they were conservative, preferring to use the cameras and enlargers with which they were most familiar. The definition obtained from large plate cameras was extremely good and, ideally suited to photographing vehicles and workshop scenes, they remained in use for many years. At Doncaster Works the mainstay was a

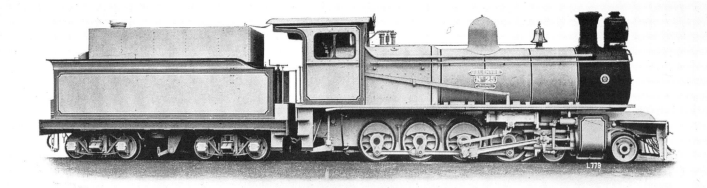

NORTH BRITISH LOCOMOTIVE COMPANY, LIMITED, GLASGOW.

For this Engine and Tender, quote Reference No. **L 779** or Code Word **ARGOLANDO.**

Gauge of Railway, 3-ft. 0-in.

TYPE 4-8-0

ENGINE.

CYLINDERS { DIAMETER ... ... 17-in.
STROKE ... ... 20-in.

WHEELS ... { BOGIE DIAMETER. ... 2-ft. 3-in.
COUPLED ., ... 3-ft. 3-in.

WHEEL-BASE { RIGID ... ... 7-ft. 2-in.
TOTAL ... ... 19-ft. 9-in.

WORKING PRESSURE ... 180-lbs. per sq. in.

BOILER FEED 2 No. 8 COMBINATION INJECTORS.

HEATING SURFACE { TUBES ... ... 1,170 sq. ft.
FIREBOX ... ... 97 ,,
TOTAL ... .. 1,267 ,,

TRACTIVE FORCE AT 75% OF BOILER PRESSURE } ... ... 20,000-lbs.

WEIGHT { IN WORKING ORDER ... 46 tons 11 cwts.
ON COUPLED WHEELS 37 ,, 8 ,,

TENDER.

WHEELS, DIAMETER ... ... 2-ft. 3-in.

WHEEL-BASE ... ... 16-ft. 0-in.

TANK CAPACITY ... .. 2,500 gallons.

OIL FUEL CAPACITY ... . 1,400 gallons.

WEIGHT, FULL ... ... 34 tons 5 cwts.

ENGINE AND TENDER.

WHEEL-BASE, TOTAL ... 46-ft. 1-in.

Private railway companies used 'works grey' photographs to advertise their vehicles and the North British Locomotive Company produced a series of cards carrying images of its locomotives and basic specifications. The 4-8-0 locomotive *Valente* was built for the Peruvian Government in 1923 for service on a 3ft gauge mineral line. Potential customers could obtain further details by quoting the order number or the code word, 'Argolando'.

NB L779

wholeplate Sanderson field camera, which lasted from October 1905, when the unit was formally established, until December 1952, when the tripod was blown over and the camera irreparably damaged. It was replaced by a Kodak Specialist Model 2 half plate camera, as larger negatives were still considered best at capturing detail. It was common for company photographers to be sent into the field equipped with 12 × 10ins or 16 × 12ins plates and one of these large field cameras, probably hired from the local photographers, Messrs. Bagshaws, can be seen in the Doncaster photograph of the Great Northern 'Atlantic' at Bawtry in June 1900 (see frontispiece). Even the 'press' photographers used wholeplate negatives long after the introduction of lighter cameras and although this meant that images were of high quality, the 'action' views they took were sometimes a little strained com-

pared with the work of the more adventurous enthusiasts armed with 35mm Leicas. Paddington and Euston photographers began to use wholeplate film negatives in the 1920s, which must have at least lightened their burdens. It certainly increased productivity, for, able to carry more negatives, they could take more photographs when covering an event. By the Second World War some photographers employed by the Southern Railway, which had one of the most advanced publicity departments, were equipped with Rolleiflex cameras and used rollfilm to record the devastation caused by bombing raids. When photograph units did finally obtain 35mm cameras, as at Doncaster in 1961 where a Lordomat SLE was purchased for taking transparencies, they were extensively used and by the 1970s the majority of works photographs was probably taken on miniature or medium format film.[23]

Although smaller film sizes meant that more photographs were taken, the post-war years saw a gradual decline in official photography, as British Railways works were 'rationalised' and many of the private builders went into liquidation. They included Beyer, Peacock, which ceased locomotive construction in 1966. Sales and closures in the 1980s meant that many photographic departments disappeared along with the works they had portrayed and increasingly the railways returned to their original practice of contracting work out to local photographers, whilst advertising was handled by agencies.

Toton, near Nottingham, was one of Britain's largest and busiest railway marshalling yards. By the time this photograph was taken in 1952 to advertise the British Transport Films' *Train Time* the yard was fully mechanised, handling over 3,000 wagons daily. The yard operated day and night, lit by floodlights, and a BTF photographer climbed one of the pylons to produce this image which vividly illustrates the scale of Toton's traffic.

BTF 1315

A British Railways Western Region local train on its way through the Rhondda in the spring of 1954. The photograph is a scene from the film *Every Valley*, a British Transport Films 'day in the life' study of transport services in this South Wales community.

BTF 2523

Privatisation in the 1980s also led to the demise of British Transport Films, an official unit that had developed a unique approach to railway photography. The BTF, a successor to the LMS and Southern Railway film units founded in the 1930s, was established in 1948 to publicise the work of the British Transport Commission. The BTF used film and photography to promote the activities of the nationalised transport concerns and to aid training for their workers. Edgar Anstey, Director of the BTF, had been schooled in the documentary movement of the 1930s and encouraged his staff to produce public information films in a wide variety of styles, both gritty and witty, often with only a tangential link with transport. They included studies of modern architecture, wildlife and art, had commentaries by poets such as John Betjeman and Laurie Lee, and brought to prominence film-makers like John Schlesinger. Stills cameramen accompanied the camera crews, photographing the film units at work, sometimes duplicating scenes from the films but also creating their own interpretations. They were distinctive photographs, and were unlike any others which originated from official departments. It is doubtful whether any works or 'press' photographer would have been sent to record the passing of an old GWR tank engine hauling a local passenger service in the Rhondda, or chosen such an unusual vantage point as in the photograph opposite, with the train seen from the rear and only half in shot, the rest of the scene taken up with a battered corrugated fence and the miners' cottages draped over the hillside in the background. Unlike most official imagery, the BTF film crews and photographers were encouraged to seek out unusual angles and offbeat subjects, resulting in dramatic shots like the mass of wagons seen from a floodlight tower in Toton depot, or the sight of British Railways' most reluctant passengers, newly-convicted prisoners boarding a train at Waterloo on the first stage of their journey to Parkhurst.

Of course, works and publicity photographers also produced their share of unconventional images, from the bizarre still life of lost property at Paddington, to the Great Eastern railwayman posed alongside tongues of leather studded with nails. Separated by time and aided only by laconic, one line entries in registers, it is difficult to know why many photographs were taken, but viewed as a whole they provide a superb record of railway operations, changing working practices and the transformation of the rural and urban landscape. In a period when there was virtually no alternative to the train for long-distance travel, the railway photographers' work touched on every social class and all manner of businesses. Their images also reveal how the railway companies saw themselves and what they considered important. Express locomotives, prestigious ships and grandiose architecture feature prominently, but the photographic departments also documented the country lorry deliveries and refreshment trolleys that all formed part of the complete service offered by the railways. The choice of subjects inevitably restricted the approach the official photographer could take, for an 'artistic' interpretation

of a new stretch of track or the construction of station lavatories would not have been welcomed by the Chief Mechanical and Civil Engineers. Nevertheless, the works photographers took great professional pride in their work and wherever possible produced arresting images, particularly in their press and publicity pictures in which they consciously followed journalistic practice. It is illuminating to contrast basic official record photographs with images produced by recognised 'art' photographers, for some of them bear comparison with the best work. Certain studies of railwaymen working on locomotives are reminiscent of the work of Lewis Hine, while many carriage print landscape photographs were clearly influenced by the pictorialist school.

The National Railway Museum is also responsible, in its own way, for producing 'official' images, for it has employed photographers since its inception in 1975. Like the works photographers, the Museum staff take record views of exhibits, construction and restoration and also provide images for reproduction in books, newspapers and magazines. Part of the studio's brief is documenting the contemporary railway scene and this has included photographing major projects such as the building of Eurostar's Waterloo International Terminal, the construction of the Channel Tunnel and the electrification of East Coast Main Line. A good working relationship with the railway operators has placed the Museum's photographers in a unique position, securing them access to areas often closed to others. However, although the NRM photographers produce 'official' images they are also able to operate with sufficient independence to cover the quirky and idiosyncratic. Lynn Patrick has been one of the few women photographers working in what has always been a male-dominated field.

London, Brighton & South Coast Railway 2-2-2 locomotive No.330 *Newhaven* was, according to E. J. Bedford's note on the negative wrapper, doing 55mph when he photographed it near Lewes in the late 1880s. Bedford's comment illustrates his enthusiasm for capturing speed.

Burtt 6488

The official viewpoint has, however, only been part of the story, for enthusiasts have photographed railways since the 1850s. Railway photography is now so often coloured by nostalgia that it is worth recalling that the earliest devotees were drawn to their subject because the railways represented the cutting edge of technology. Some photographers, like Keene and Warwick, were interested in the railway landscape too, but the majority were attracted by the locomotives and wanted to produce images which portrayed the true nature of these living, breathing machines. By the end of the nineteenth century they were the fastest man-made objects, regularly reaching speeds approaching 90mph, and arresting motion became a major preoccupation for some photographers.

The photographers were at first restricted by the slow emulsions on glass plates, but in the 1880s the first amateurs, bored with static views of locomotives in stations and sheds, began to record moving trains. This was made possible by more sensitive emulsions and faster camera shutters. It is difficult to establish who took the first photograph of a train moving at speed, for several men were experimenting with the subject at the same time. The Reverend A. H. Malan, vicar of Altarnun in Cornwall, and Roger Langdon, the stationmaster at Silverton in Devon, both began to photograph the Great Western Railway's broad gauge trains in the 1880s. Dr. Tice F. Budden, encouraged by the Great Northern Railway's Superintendent of the Line, took his first railway images whilst a Cambridge undergraduate in 1889, and was one of the earliest photographers to attempt panning, following the moving train with his camera to 'freeze' the motion, producing a blurred background in the process.

Budden's contemporary at Cambridge, P. W. Pilcher, was also fascinated by movement and spent hours at the lineside, photographing passing trains. Like many who followed him, Pilcher was not interested in speed alone, for he most enjoyed photographing trains at Whitmore, the top of a steep gradient on the London & North Western Railway's line between Crewe and Stafford, where the locomotives were working at their hardest, producing clouds of smoke and steam as evidence of their efforts.[24] Speed was a factor in some of Pilcher's most memorable images. He was a music master at Shrewsbury School and was in the town on 15th October 1907 to photograph the horrific aftermath of the derailment of the West of England Night Mail. It had inexplicably approached the sharp curve into the station at about 75mph, killing eighteen passengers and crew.

E. J. Bedford, an art teacher from Lewes, began his photographic career with landscapes, buildings and natural history, but he became engrossed by the technical demands of railway photography and particularly halting motion. He devoted considerable efforts to photographing locomotives of the London, Brighton & South Coast Railway, typically seen in head-on or threequarter views to reduce the blurring effects of speed as in the photograph on page 23. Like many pioneer railway photographers, Bedford's work was not widely recognised by the

broader photographic community at the time, because his images were circulated almost exclusively amongst other enthusiasts.[25] Obviously, the portrayal of locomotives at speed was not just left to independent amateurs and publicity-conscious railway managers soon asked their company photographers to produce similar views. The Great Western's men created striking images of speeding express trains near Bath, but perhaps the most dramatic nineteenth century photograph is the picture of the LNWR engine *Jeanie Deans* picking up water at Bushey Troughs in 1899. It is a shot from a film made by the British Mutoscope & Biograph Co. Ltd. and was taken from a camera mounted on a special train running on a parallel track to the express.[26] The sensation of movement is heightened because the photograph is slightly blurred, the locomotive and tender wreathed in smoke, steam and cascades of water. This was an effect amateur photographers were often reluctant to reproduce. As lighter cameras and sensitive emulsions became available the best photographers, using their carefully refined

The aftermath of a serious accident, the cause of which was never wholly determined. In the early hours of 15th October 1907 a London & North Western Railway mail train from Crewe to the west approached Shrewsbury station at 75mph as the crew tried to regain time lost at the beginning of the journey. The train failed to stop at signals and was derailed on a section of line subject to a 10mph speed restriction. The locomotive crew, two guards, three Post Office sorters and eleven passengers were killed. This photograph, taken on the morning of the disaster by local schoolmaster P. W. Pilcher, shows the locomotive, 'Experiment' class No.2052 *Stephenson* amidst the wreckage.

Burtt 6217

techniques, could stop movement dead. These men usually preferred their photographs to clearly show details of the wheels, cylinders and valve gear at the expense of conveying the impression of speed. Their approach resulted in excellent record shots, but when viewed *en masse* they can seem stilted and repetitious, so photographs like the image of *Jeanie Deans* are comparatively rare.

In its formative years photography was almost exclusively the preserve of the wealthy. Cameras and negatives were expensive and few working men or women had the leisure time to visit suitable locations and then process and print their plates or film. This probably explains why so many of the early railway photographers were doctors, teachers and clergymen. They were predominantly amateurs, but as railway publishing for a general audience took off at the end of the nineteenth century the more enterprising were presented with ways of defraying the costs of their hobby and of supplying images to those who were unable to afford their own cameras.

The F. Moore Company was founded by two railway fanatic brothers apprenticed to the Great Eastern Railway, A. and A. R. Morton Bell. In 1896, joined by a third brother, they commenced publication of *Moore's Monthly Magazine*, later to be known as *The Locomotive*. The magazine drew on the growing archive of photographs sold to them by men such as Budden and was marketed to a new phenomenon, the 'railwayists'.[27]

Sales were also encouraged by the postcard craze, particularly after the Morton Bells had, in 1900, established the Locomotive Publishing Company. The LPC produced both printed and photographic reproductions of railway images. Some of the most unusual required the photographers' collaboration with Thomas Rudd, an artist who signed himself 'F. Moore'. He specialised in painted photographs, working in oils on partially exposed prints, accurately rendering colours but sometimes removing unwanted details, such as telegraph poles, trees or permanent way gangs. Rudd was a prolific artist, cre-

The London & North Western Railway locomotive *Jeanie Deans* picking up water at Bushey Troughs in 1899, a shot from a film made by the British Mutoscope & Biograph Co. Ltd. The photographers were on a parallel track, on a special train which made several unsuccessful attempts to match the speed of their subject before they produced this spectacular image.

Crewe C 541

ating two or three paintings a week which were published in the railway press or reproduced as postcards. The widespread sales they enjoyed demonstrated how deeply railway imagery had penetrated public consciousness.[28] The growth of the railway press encouraged photographers to indulge their hobby and although in the early years of the twentieth century the standards of reproduction were rarely high, the published images provided a bench mark by which new work could be judged. However, catering for a market which was far more interested in railways than photography, the magazine and postcard publishers restricted experimentation, posing limitations on style and demanding that all images showed the whole of a train, not just the locomotive and tender.[29]

Many photographers who merely wanted a technical record of the vehicles they had seen were content to take simple shots of inactive locomotives in sidings and sheds. A Manchester dentist, W. H. Whitworth, set himself the virtually impossible task of photographing each of the main railway companies' engines and although the results were static views which demonstrated little effort to show the environment in which they worked, Whitworth did produce hundreds of images of locomotives which would otherwise have been ignored. For some photographers the thrill of the chase was all and these men did not even take the trouble to print their negatives, preferring to roam the network in search of engines they had not previously encountered. Others took a more systematic approach. H. Gordon Tidey, who sold many of his negatives to the commercial outlets, from the age of twenty-one devoted one week a year to photography, covering much of England and Scotland. Unlike many photographers he did not have a favourite railway company, but he did return time after time to preferred locations, such as Dillicar Troughs on the LNWR's main route north, and he particularly enjoyed his days at Carlisle station, where in the early 1900s he could photograph locomotives from seven different companies from the same spot.[30]

Despite advances in camera and negative technology, photographers like Tidey were still hampered by the limited range of specialised equipment available. Few enthusiasts could afford the large plate cameras favoured by the official photographers and in any case they were so heavy that they made travel to the best rural locations virtually impossible. Most favoured reflex or press cameras with smaller $4\frac{1}{4} \times 3\frac{1}{4}$ins quarter plate glass negatives, as these lightened their load a little, but Tidey and others continued to work with larger half-plates. The camera shutters were often inefficient and needed regular attention if they were to work at the correct speeds, and all but the most affluent photographers had to be content with lenses with apertures no wider than f6.8.[31] By the 1930s many photographers, like Eric Treacy and Maurice Earley, fitted their cameras with swing fronts, which compensated for differences in focus between near and distant objects and could blur backgrounds when required. The swing front improved sharpness, but slowed the action of the camera, so some photographers, E. R. Wethersett amongst them, rejected them. Bellows cameras, after regular use, also began to show signs of wear, letting in little pinpricks of light marking or fogging negatives which then had to be carefully retouched.

Even the most accomplished photographers usually claimed that they did not aim to create images of great artistic merit and that they were only concerned with making a factual record, but many were clearly interested in more than that.[32] They invested in expensive equipment — the Thornton Pickard f4.5 reflex camera, popular in the 1920s and used by many enthusiasts, cost £12 10s (£12.50) at a time when a newly-qualified engine driver could expect to earn about 12s a day (60p)[33] — and devoted much of their spare time to railway photography. Many adopted complex strategies to ensure that each day's work brought a suitable haul of locomotives and they meticulously planned many of their most dramatic images. J. E. Simpson, who began photographing railways with a Kodak Box Brownie at the age of ten, claimed to have adopted the methodical approach of the stamp collector, cycling across the London & South Western Railway's operating area until he had 'collected' all that company's locomotives.[34]

In the days before widespread car ownership most photographers travelled by train or bicycle and so images of the most remote rural lines are rare. In the 1920s Maurice Earley, hampered by a lack of transport and limited holidays, took to photographing trains passing near his home town of Reading and soon learned how to exploit the local weather, light and operating conditions to greatest effect. He chose the Reading West to Southcote Junction line because it ran from north to south, where the sun could be positioned behind the photographer at an angle of 45° and the prevailing wind blew smoke away from the camera. His other favoured location was Sonning Cutting, more problematic for it was on the main Paddington to Bristol line, running from east to west, and the sun was only in the best position for the briefest period. Here, however, the steep embankments offered some protection from the wind's influence on the engine's smoke and Earley soon discovered that he could use the road bridges and trees to shade his lens from direct sunlight. He returned to Sonning Cutting again and again, and there took some of the most majestic photographs of Great Western locomotives and the diesels that followed them. Earley enjoyed photographing trains at speed, particularly on showery days in the spring or autumn with skies enlivened by cloud which reflected light into the shadow areas. He enhanced clouds on the negative through the use of filters, but would never use "fake" skies by double printing from other negatives and rather than asking footplate crews to make smoke for the camera, chose to photograph on gradients or speed restricted areas where the fireman piled on coal.[35]

Purists were as concerned with locomotive technology as photography and viewed some of the more creative techniques as anathema, for although nearly all of them liked spectacular speed photographs they expected these images to be an objective record of locomotive performance. In the 1930s and 1940s Dr. Pat Ransome-Wallis even used retouching ink to remove smoke from his negatives if they showed evidence of poor running or sloppy firing and applied iodo-cyanide reducer to prints to blank out skies. Ransome-Wallis at first was not worried about the loss of a few clouds and was content to obtain a good "studio portrait" of both sides of every class of locomotive, with a record of major modifications and a shot of it 'on train'. In his later career, however, he incorporated skies, smoke and steam into his images to oblige editors and consequently they were widely published.

Eric Treacy, one of the band of railway fanatic clergymen, professed that many of his best smoke effects were pre-arranged with footplatemen whom he befriended in the engine sheds.[36] He also believed that careful planning was essential for good photography and made mental notes of suitable viewpoints whenever he travelled by train. He chose his sites for their scenic beauty, the locomotives which used the routes and the way in which they "handled", and with regard to the position of the sun and likely temperature. Sparing in his use of film, Treacy decided that he would take no photographs until he reached his desired location and once there would even ignore passing trains if the locomotives were not performing exactly as he wished.[37] Treacy, who began railway photography in 1929, took his hobby seriously and was as well equipped as many full-time professionals. He often carried three cameras and a tripod on his journeys, exposing glass negatives in a quarter-plate Soho Reflex and a 9 × 12cm

Zeiss Contessa Press Camera, and rollfilm in his Zeiss Super Ikonta. The folding German cameras and the medium format Hasselblad and Rolleiflex became increasingly popular in the late-1930s and, comparatively lightweight with shutter speeds of 1/500 second, they made stopping movement much easier. They were still expensive, but gradually serious photography was becoming affordable.

Treacy's superior photography secured him membership of the Railway Photographic Society, which had been founded in 1922 by Maurice Earley. One of the Society's main aims was to improve the standard of railway images so members regularly circulated their work for criticism by their peers. This resulted in photographs of a very high calibre, but at times a fear of censure seems to have encouraged the members to produce immaculate studies of passing trains with little attempt at variety. On one criticism sheet returned to Cyril Herbert after he had forwarded a distant view of a train passing Occupation Crossing in Cambridgeshire, members commented "not a train shot" and asked "Why not by the side of the line in a spot like this? Are you sure it was not taken from the doorway of a local inn?"[38] Even Treacy, who complained that constant repetition of threequarters views was "rather tedious", exercised a form of self censorship, for like many other members of the Society he took no railway photographs at all between November and March.[39] With the exception of a few snow scenes poor weather hardly ever features in many huge private collections which represent thousands of hours spent at the lineside, and there are few photographic equivalents of 'Rain, Wind and Speed'. Many photographers, too, focussed almost exclusively on main line express services, ignoring inelegant freight trains and even refusing to photograph dirty locomotives. This could bring its own problems. Maurice Earley had to carefully 'burn in' the tops of Great Western engines' boilers when printing, because the cleaners' polishing had made them so reflective that they hardly registered on his negatives. It is worth recalling too, that when the majority of images were taken on expensive glass plates each exposure had to count. Earley, who throughout his long affair with the railways used glass negatives almost exclusively, explained that he only ever had enough holders for six plates and so had to exercise great self-discipline, knowing that once these had been used it was time to return home.[40]

The 35mm film camera, introduced into Britain in 1925 when the first Leicas were imported from Germany, was slow to catch on amongst railway photographers, who preferred the quality which larger negatives usually guaranteed. Both Ransome-Wallis and Treacy returned to reflex and press cameras after fleeting trials of miniature film. The Leicas were convenient, but it was difficult to retouch the negatives with 'Photopake' and they were sometimes a little grainy. Cyril Herbert, however, who had started photographing railways with his boyhood Box Brownie, persisted. His obsession brought him to work for the LNER and he remained with the railways for the rest of his working life. He found that he could carry lightweight 35mm cameras with him at all times, allowing him to take photographs on train journeys, from his office window at King's Cross or when supervising work on the line. He believed that a "really good railway picture" required sunshine, a clean locomotive and exhaust smoke, but the conditions he worked under meant that his photographs were often taken "on the spur of the moment", in poor weather or with the sun in the 'wrong' position.[41] The locations were rarely those favoured by fellow enthusiasts and the locomotives were sometimes portrayed hauling dirty goods wagons or humdrum commuter trains, for he felt that it was not just the fast services which made powerful images. Herbert, as well as joining the Railway Photographic Society, was a member of the Leica Postal Portfolio group and so submitted his work to the wider photographic community for comment. These images, chosen to appeal to people with little or no interest in railways, disclosed a concern for abstract forms or subjects which were largely overlooked by the more conventional enthusiasts and included photographs of the footplate crews and the permanent way gangs who worked on the lines.

Herbert's special skills meant that his photographs were sometimes used by his employers, particularly during the Second World War when he contributed part of the official record of war damage on LNER lines and property in and around London. The railway companies, however, usually had an equivocal attitude towards photography by 'amateurs'. A schoolboy, George Tod, describes in a letter written to his brother in the 1890s how he sought permission to take photographs from Robert Weatherburn, the Midland Railway London District Superintendent at Kentish Town: "I presented myself tremblingly at his door, which was opened after some time by . . . a man encircled in a cloud of smoke (who) thumped up and yelled at me what I wanted so I . . . told him plainly what I wanted at first he shook his head and said not but then he . . . said they did not allow that sort of thing then he said I would not interfere with the drivers or anybody so I informed him that statement was correct so he said he thought he could allow me and then he said he would allow me . . .".[42] After this forbidding introduction Weatherburn proved very accommodating and even posed for Tod alongside the locomotives under his care. On occasion, too, the railway companies could be generous in issuing passes which permitted photographers to cross their boundaries to work at the lineside. Maurice Earley's photographs, for example, were much admired at the GWR's Paddington headquarters and the company granted him access to Sonning Cutting and other lines near Reading. Godfrey Soole, however, who in the 1930s produced a series of photographs of the GWR's services in the Bath and Bristol area, ended his hobby abruptly in 1938, the year he joined the company as a traffic manager. Soole's photographs, mainly threequarters views of speeding passenger trains, are far from controversial and could have done no more harm to the GWR's image than Maurice Earley's classic views. Yet the GWR, anxious to maintain complete control over its public face, discouraged photography by its employees. In Soole's case this was a great pity, for in the six years or so that he was

The schoolboy photographer George Tod went to considerable pains to build up his collection of locomotive photographs, braving the wrath of company officials, shed foremen and footplate crews to obtain permission to indulge his hobby. Tod must have possessed a certain charm, for in general they seem to have been very obliging and even the daunting Robert Weatherburn, the Midland Railway London District Superintendent at Kentish Town, posed for him with a '2183' class 4-4-0 locomotive at St. Pancras.

Tod 49

---

active he produced some excellent images.

In the Second World War there was little private photography, as shortage of film and security restrictions prevented enthusiasts from venturing on to the railways. With a few exceptions, therefore, our record of their role in the conflict is that of the company photographers, who produced publicity images which accorded with the Government's censorship policies. Nationalisation of the railways in 1948 gave photographers new challenges, for enthusiasts were always interested in seeing engines on the 'wrong lines'. That year's locomotive exchanges provided them with countless opportunities, as the new British Railways carried out trials on the locomotives which it inherited. Some photographers, like Treacy, Coles, Herbert and Earley, were able to sell their photographs to the official departments, who used them in their publicity. However, with increasing competition from roads, the passing of the Clean Air Acts in the 1950s and a steady conversion from steam to diesel and electric traction, it became clear to photographers that they were now recording the end of an era. Herbert, for example, regretted his tendency to concentrate on the newest and grandest engines, and in the post-war years decided to photograph the oldest vehicles whilst they were still working.[43] Others, like Kenneth Leech, rediscovered their interest in railways, reasoning that the industry was changing so rapidly that they felt compelled to record it.[44]

A classic Maurice Earley photograph, which he titled 'Majesty in Motion'. It features the Great Western Railway locomotive *King Richard I* near Reading West with the 'Cornish Riviera Limited' service from London to Penzance on 18th April 1938. Circumstances combined to provide Earley with a "ready-made opportunity" for this shot. Work on an underbridge meant that the train was restricted to just 15mph, making it easier to arrest motion, while the weather was sunny, with a northerly wind that blew the smoke and steam upwards. The locomotive and carriages were all in pristine condition. Earley claimed that although he returned to the same spot on many occasions he could never repeat this scene.

Earley 3600

Colour photography came within the reach of the serious amateur in 1934, with the introduction of Dufaycolour transparency film. The first colour films were exclusively available in large format and as their slow emulsions meant that they were only suited to static subjects, they were not widely used by railway photographers. It proved very difficult to obtain colour film during the Second World War, but in the early 1950s Kodachrome transparency film appeared on the market in a range of formats. Nevertheless, many railway photographers were reluctant to abandon black and white film, which was cheaper, allowed greater latitude for exposure errors and could be used in poor light or with rapid shutter speeds. They could also process and print black and white negatives in a simple home darkroom, maintaining control over the whole procedure from start to finish. Gradually, however, enthusiasts began to carry additional cameras loaded with colour film. The most serious photographers preferred transparency film, particularly if they hoped to see their images in print, for it was best suited to reproduction. Professionals too began to use colour for publicity work, as the public came to expect colour photographs in glossy brochures and posters. In the 1960s and 1970s cheap processing and printing became commonplace and many enthusiasts turned to colour negative film. Today colour film is used for most railway photographs.

The prime attraction of the railways for most enthusiasts was steam and as it disappeared from main line passenger services they diverted their attention to branch lines and took an increasing interest in freight traffic. The imminent withdrawal of steam and the implementation of Dr. Beeching's notorious report, *The Reshaping of British Railways*, provoked many enthusiasts to take up the camera. With good quality equipment within the reach of most pockets, the 1960s was probably the most active decade for railway photography. Car ownership was commonplace, allowing photographers to reach even the most remote locations and the most threatened and picturesque routes, such as the Settle to Carlisle line, became increasingly popular. Now, an industry which had once lured the camera because it represented the very latest in technology was photographed with a conscious air of nostalgia. To a certain extent this was nothing new, as even in the 1850s Bleasdale had been keen to document the final days of the first locomotives and in 1892 the Great Western photographers had sadly recorded the reluctant conversion to broad gauge and the scrapping of obsolete engines. Yet by the 1960s, when British Railways had built its last steam locomotive, when stations were being demolished and track torn up, it was obvious that photographic opportunities would never be the same. Some photographers, of course, took an interest in the new vehicles, but most of the best photographs of these new services were taken by official units, working to the instructions of advertising and publicity managers. With the exception, perhaps, of the 'Deltics', the prosaic diesel and electric locomotives seem not to have inspired a great deal of affection, for it has never been as easy to create an image of a multiple unit as spectacular as a photograph of even the most humble steam-powered freight locomotive at work.

Many photographers, like E. R. Wethersett, lost interest in railways with the demise of steam on British Railways in 1968. Some of the best, Eric Treacy among them, soldiered on using the skills they had perfected in glass plate days to produce marvellous images of modern traction at favourite locations. Others travelled increasingly further afield, to Eastern Europe and China, where steam still operated and the settings were more exotic. These journeys were sometimes made with a degree of risk, as Dr. Ransome-Wallis discovered when he was arrested on several occasions for spying and was forced to dodge coal hurled by an irate driver in Czechoslovakia.

Not content with perpetuating steam on film, some photographers became actively involved in the rescue of historic vehicles from scrap yards and ensured that they not only survived, but were restored to working order. Patrick Whitehouse and John Adams were keen photographers who also made *Railway Roundabout*, a series of BBC films which chronicled the final days of country branch lines. They went on to play major roles in founding the Talyllyn Railway and the Birmingham Railway Museum. A flourishing preservation movement in Britain has encouraged many photographers to devote their attentions to historic locomotives rather than recording the contemporary scene. The technical standard is often high and the images pleasing to the eye, but too many of them are attempts to recreate a world which in truth never existed.

Nearly all the enthusiasts were drawn to their subject by a love of the technology and inevitably this is what features most strongly in their work. Few have ever shown much interest in people, so the countless millions who have laboured and travelled by rail are sadly absent from most 'private' photographs. Where people do appear in these images they are usually railway workers, particularly the signalmen, main-

A couple relax on a station bench at Boat of Garten station in the Highlands. The station served both the London, Midland & Scottish and London & North Eastern Railways, and LNER D41 class 4-4-0 locomotive No.6904 is waiting to depart with a passenger train. This snapshot by J. M. Crowther is far from typical of his work, for he mainly concentrated on passing locomotives photographed from the lineside.

Crowther 4/41

tenance gangs and footplate crews befriended by men like Treacy, Herbert and Burtt. Photographs of passengers are very rare, except as incidental figures in the background and scenes such as Crowther's delightful snapshot of the couple waiting on a bench at Boat of Garten are hardly typical of the private photographers' output. This means that for the depiction of what it was like to journey by rail we must turn to official images. They are fine photographs, but they were nearly always taken to emphasise the railway's good points. As a consequence they were rarely subtle and can hardly be considered as objective records. Awed by powerful locomotives and speeding express trains, the private photographers in their way inadvertently acted as propagandists for the railways. The difficult task of conveying the boredom, frustration and overcrowding that for many has represented the authentic experience of rail travel has been left to independent photographers working to different agendas.

Railway architecture, too, had its adherents, but these were comparatively few when compared with the devotees of mechanical engineering. The most grandiose building projects were best recorded by the railway concerns, which could arrange special access or employ the services of experts such

as H. Bedford Lemere. There was, however, a small body of enthusiasts, such as Sherlock, Norman and Mowat, who took an interest in vernacular building styles and they travelled the system to photograph stations and goods depots. Other photographers, like Treacy, Earley and Click, learned to exploit station architecture to enhance their portraits of locomotives. They set expresses below grandiose station roofs, local trains at tranquil rural stations and, a particular favourite, resting steam engines in smoky roundhouses, light streaming in through the skylights. The destruction of the 1960s brought a bustle of activity, as buildings were closed, converted or, like Euston's Doric portico and Great Hall, demolished. Now photographs are all that remain of many imposing structures which once featured so prominently in the Victorians' pioneering images.

150 years of railway photography have left a unique legacy of images. They range from mundane technical records to the spectacular and the beautiful. The distinctive vision of the photographers has shaped the way the world views the railway's great machines, grand structures and, of course, its workers and passengers. Many of the best are in the photographic collections of the National Railway Museum.

Ed Bartholomew

References

1. C. C. B. Herbert, *My Best Railway Photographs*, Ian Allan, 1947, p.3.
2. K. H. Vignoles, *Charles Blacker Vignoles: Romantic Engineer*, Cambridge University Press, 1982, p.164.
3. Jack Simmons, *Image of the Train*, National Museum of Photography, Film & Television, 1993, p.12.
4. M. Butlin & E. Joll, *The Paintings of J. M. W. Turner*, p.256-7, quoted in Jack Simmons, *The Victorian Railway*, Thames & Hudson, 1991, p.127.
5. *The Locomotive Magazine*, Vol 30, 15 August 1924, pp.249-50.
6. *The Engineer*, Volume 1, 20 June 1856, quoted in R. L. Hills & D. Patrick, *Beyer, Peacock, Locomotive Builders to the World*, Transport Publishing Company, 1982, p.43.
7. Information supplied by Brian Radford, and in Maxwell Craven, *Keene's Derby*, Breedon Books, 1992, pp.24-27.
8. Brian Radford, *Derby Works and Midland Railway Locomotives*, Ian Allan, 1971, p.73.
9. W. M. Acworth, *The Railways of England*, William Clowes, 1889, p.179.
10. T. A. Scotton, 'The Work of a Railway Photographer' in *LMS Railway Magazine*, July 1927, p.226.
11. *The British Journal of Photography*, 13 January 1893, p.25.
12. Scott Damant, 'Art in Railway Carriages' in *The Railway Magazine*, February 1898, p.159.
13. op cit, p.164.
14. 'L.C.' in *LMS Magazine*, March 1938, p.106.
15. *The Railway Gazette*, 19 February 1937, p.12.
16. Greg Norden, *Landscapes Under the Luggage Rack*, Great Norden Railway Publications, 1997, p.34.
17. W. H. Jarvis, 'The Great Western Railway Guide "Holiday Haunts"', *Great Western Railway Magazine*, March 1933, p.114.
18. T. B. Russell, *Commercial Advertising*, quoted in Jack Simmons, *The Victorian Railway*, Thames & Hudson, 1991, p.258.
19. 'L.C.' in *LMS Magazine*, June 1932, p.238.
20. Retirement Notice in *LMS Magazine*, July 1932, p.238.
21. Information supplied by Brian Radford.
22. T. A. Scotton, 'The Work of a Railway Photographer' in *LMS Railway Magazine*, July 1927, p.229.
23. Note in photographic register, *Doncaster Large Glass Plate Negatives, 1897-1967*, NRM 1997-7396.
24. Jack Simmons, *Image of the Train*, National Museum of Photography, Film & Television, 1993, p.23.
25. John Minnis, *E. J. Bedford of Lewes, Photographer of the London, Brighton & South Coast Railway*, Wild Swan, 1989.
26. *The Locomotive Magazine*, Vol 4, September 1899, p.145.
27. Jack Simmons, *Image of the Train*, National Museum of Photography, Film & Television, 1993, p.25.
28. V. R. Webster, 'F. Moore, the story of a notable railway artist' in *Railway World*, Volume 45, November 1984, pp.584-91.
29. H. Gordon Tidey, *Those Were the Trains*, Ian Allan, 1957, p.7.
30. op cit.
31. op cit.
32. For example Maurice Earley, *The Great Western Scene*, Oxford Publishing Company, 1970, p.2.
33. *National Agreement in Regard to Railway Staff*, Railway Staff Conference, 1921, p.393.
34. Information supplied by J. E. Simpson.
35. Maurice Earley, *My Best Railway Photographs*, Ian Allan, 1946, pp.3-7.
36. Eric Treacy, *My Best Railway Photographs*, Ian Allan, 1946, p.4.
37. Eric Treacy, *Still More of my Best Railway Photographs*, Ian Allan, 1948.
38. Railway Photographic Society Criticism Sheet, dated 10 June 1937, in NRM 1997-7218.
39. Eric Treacy, *Still More of My Best Railway Photographs*, Ian Allan, 1948, p.4.
40. Maurice Earley, *Truly the Great Western*, Oxford Publishing Company, 1975, p.4.
41. C. C. B. Herbert, *My Best Railway Photographs*, Ian Allan, 1947, p.4.
42. From letters in NRM 1996-7817, quoted in Amba Kumar, 'Gems from the Collection', *FNRM Newsletter*, February 1997, p.10.
43. C. C. B. Herbert, *More of my Best Railway Photographs*, Ian Allan, 1948, p.3.
44. Interview in *Steam Railway*, No 116, December 1989, p.48.

Amongst the first railway photographs were views of major engineering projects, such as the construction of I.K. Brunel's Royal Albert Bridge linking Devon and Cornwall, which features in this albumen print of 1858. The first span is almost in position and the second has been floated into the River Tamar from the Devon shore. The spans were painstakingly raised by hydraulic rams while the stone piers were built up to the trusses three feet at a time.

Clapham   847/62

A Great Western 4-2-2 locomotive speeds past Uphill Junction in Somerset with the down 'Cornishman' bound for Penzance in this photograph by the Reverend A. H. Malan. The signalman, leaning from his box, signals with a flag, while a permanent way gang rest on the grassy embankment. Malan noted that a train to Weston-super-Mare had just passed, "leaving behind a smoky atmosphere", and it is just visible in the distance.

LPC   50412

Shafts of light shine through the Gothic windows of William Henry Barlow's St. Pancras station, photographed for the Midland Railway as it neared completion in 1868.

NRM   1079/80

The magnificent roof of St. Pancras station, seen as construction reached its conclusion in 1868. This albumen print was made from a 12 × 10ins wet collodion glass plate. The unknown photographer sensitised the plate, probably in a portable darkroom, and then climbed to the top of the scaffolding, carrying a bulky camera and tripod. The wet plate was exposed before it could dry and then the photographer returned as quickly as possible to ground level where he developed, fixed and washed the negative.

NRM   1080/80

In August 1876 a party of
seventeen wealthy tourists,
accompanied by two maid-
servants, a cook and a
steward, set out on a 26 day
mystery tour of the British
Isles, from St. Pancras to the
West Country, Derbyshire,
on to Scotland and back
again. Travelling in the
luxury of the newly-
introduced Pullman cars,
they journeyed along some
of the most scenic railway
routes in Britain, including
the newly-built Settle to
Carlisle line.

NRM   9/98

Guests of the Great Central
Railway at the official
opening ceremony of
Immingham Dock performed
by King George V on 22nd
July 1912. It is one of a
series of platinum
photographic prints
recording the construction of
the docks, compiled for the
General Manager of the
Great Central Railway, Sam
Fay.

1442/63/3

Navvies mix concrete under the supervision of their foreman during the building of London's Metropolitan Railway in the early 1860s. The line's engineer, John Fowler, commissioned a series of photographs recording the construction of the line, the world's first underground railway.

Clapham   1478/23/63

The early photographers' interest in railways often extended beyond views of locomotives and the construction of new lines. Here, navvies working on the building of the LNWR and Midland's joint colliery lines in Leicestershire in the early 1870s celebrate a Gala Day with a barrow race at Bosworth, watched by local dignitaries. The long exposure required has blurred the rippling flags and the movements of the onlookers.

Contr/11

When he took up photography in the middle years of the nineteenth century, R. H. Bleasdale knew that some of the earliest locomotives had already been scrapped and he set himself the task of recording those that remained before they were lost forever. *Adelaide* was built in 1832 by Stephenson & Co. for the Stockton & Darlington Railway. It was serving as a stationary engine driving a mortar mill during the construction of the Zetland Hotel in Saltburn when Bleasdale photographed it in about 1860.

Clapham   4854/47Y

The arrival of the railways gave a great boost to seaside resorts and holiday traffic became an important source of passenger revenue. The delights of Whitby's sands in about 1900 are advertised in this panoramic view by A. H. Robinson which once decorated the carriages of the North Eastern Railway.

Miscalb   125/43

"The evidence of the sun": two North Eastern Railway 0-6-0 locomotives derailed in an accident on an embankment between Winston and Gainford in County Durham on 24th October 1905. The accident was caused by workmen who had removed a length of rail. The photograph was part of a record compiled by the locomotive engineer, Edward Thompson, when he worked with the NER's running department.

Miscalb   110/4

The British locomotive building industry expanded rapidly in the latter half of the nineteenth century and cultivated a thriving export market. Locomotive No.690, built in 1883 by Neilson & Co. of Glasgow for the Chemin de fer de l'Ouest is being loaded on board ship at Newhaven en route to France.

Clapham   1238/63

Cyanotypes are more usually associated with fine art photography but the Stratford Works official photographers made cheap cyanotype reference prints from their negatives. This view is of a Class B12 locomotive with the Continental boat train at Seven Arch Bridge, near Brentwood, in 1925.

Stratford SX 838

Budden's photograph of a Lancashire & Yorkshire Railway Liverpool to Manchester express on Walkden Troughs in 1900 was used as the basis of a painting. Applying paint directly to a lightly exposed print, the artist, Thomas Rudd, removed unwanted features like the permanent way gang standing at the side of the line and sharpened the slightly blurred outline of the locomotive. The painting was reproduced as a postcard in Tuck's 'Famous Expresses' series and met the public's demand for colour images before the advent of colour photography. Rudd and fellow artists who worked in his studio signed their works 'F. Moore'. Black and white photographic prints from Budden's original negative were later sold by Locomotive and General Railway Photographs.

LGRP 21245

LIVERPOOL-MANCHESTER EXPRESS
LANCASHIRE & YORKSHIRE RLY.

Three young ladies and the station staff obligingly pose for the Nottingham photographer A. W. Cox on the newly-completed Kirklington station in 1871. The photograph was taken on the instructions of the contractor, John Bayliss, who included it in an album recording his firm's role in the construction of the Mansfield to Southwell line. He presented a copy to the Institution of Civil Engineers, explaining how photography could inform and inspire its members.

Miscalb   128/23

Graphically illustrating the changes the railways brought to the pace of life, a donkey cart passes as navvies pause in their work on the skew bridge at Harpenden. The photograph was taken during the Midland Railway's widening of the Chiltern Green to Elstree line in 1893.

Briggs   60

This Hurman International 10 × 8ins plate camera was purchased by the North Eastern Railway Carriage & Wagon Department Drawing Office to photograph newly-completed vehicles at York works. It is typical of the large format cameras used for many years by official photographic units and is part of the National Railway Museum's collections.

NRM 1647/85

There are few images of the official photographers at work, but the Caledonian Railway's man left his shadow at the corner of this view of a 12-ton bogie trolley wagon in 1900. The heavy plate camera is mounted on a tripod.

SRX 357

New locomotives were specially painted in 'works grey' for photography and the advantages of this treatment are apparent in these two views of newly-completed London & North Western Railway locomotives at Crewe Works. This finish included a flat paint, with 'brightwork' picked out in white, which is reproduced to good effect in both of these images.

These locomotives were produced to the design of Francis William Webb, Locomotive Superintendent of the London & North Western Railway from 1871 to 1903 and were examples of his unconventional approach. 2-(2-2)-0 No.310 *Sarmatian*, built at Crewe in 1884, is one of Webb's 'Experiment' class, which featured two high-pressure outside cylinders and a low-pressure inside cylinder driving the rear and forward wheels respectively. Webb himself is seen standing on the footplate of the brand-new *Greater Britain* on 9th October 1891.

Crewe B23

The lavish interior of the saloon built for the Prince of Wales by the London & North Western Railway in the 1880s. The glass plate camera and tripod have been inadvertently captured in the image, reflected in the mirror at the end of the carriage. Producing views of carriage interiors was an important feature of the works photographers' job, although few carriages were decorated in such an opulent style.

Crewe A84

London & North Western Railway Class G 0-8-0 locomotive No.2653 photographed at Crewe Works on 23rd March 1910. To provide a white surround the image was masked with a piece of card glued to the negative, roughly shaped to fit around the locomotive. The fine detail of the background immediately surrounding the engine was then removed with retouching ink. Only the main subject appeared on the publicity prints.

Crewe B 133

At the London & North Western Railway's Crewe Works a specially-erected screen provided a white backdrop for official photographs. It appears in this image taken at the same location as the photograph above. The photograph, dated 25th January 1912, records the completion of the 0-8-2 shunting engine No.289.

Crewe B 149

Streamlining was the epitome of transport style in the 1930s. *Coronation*, the first of the London, Midland & Scottish Railway's streamlined express passenger locomotives built for the renowned 'Coronation Scot' service from London to Scotland, was pictured in 'works grey' at Derby on 15th May 1937. The locomotive was finished in distinctive blue and silver livery with matching carriages.

Derby 22443

The Photographic Studio at Derby Works in June 1914. The building housed a dark room, two rooms used for enlarging outsized prints, a 'true to scale' room where drawings were copied, a toning room and offices. The conservatory, with its natural lighting, was used for portraiture, photographing objects, retouching and daylight printing.

Derby 10221

Photographic assistants mounting and retouching prints in the studio at Derby Works copied from the *LMS Railway Magazine* of June 1927. Working at her easel, an assistant retouches a photograph of an 0-6-0 locomotive in 'works grey', whilst her colleagues mount finished prints.

NRM 168/97

Looking like the ribcage of a beached whale, this unusual photograph was taken at Yarrow Works in Glasgow. It shows the high-pressure water tube boiler of the W1 class 4-6-4 compound locomotive No.10000, built by the London & North Eastern Railway and completed in 1929. This unconventional design was contracted out by the LNER and Yarrow provided the company with prints recording the manufacture of the boiler.

NRM 172/84

An arresting photograph, but it was taken purely for record purposes. It shows flaws in the wheel of a Great Eastern Railway locomotive which was serviced at Stratford Works. Recording flaws, fractures and damaged components for the railway companies' engineering departments was an important, if routine, part of the official photographers' duties.

Stratford 1139

F. E. Mackay poses for his friend and fellow photographer Maurice Earley in 1924, at Greenwood signal box near Hadley Wood tunnel, on the London & North Eastern Railway's main line north from King's Cross. Mackay's folding glass plate camera is mounted on a tripod and is typical of the bulky equipment railway photographers carried in the years before the Second World War.

Earley F1A/30

Six members of the Railway Photographic Society pictured by the Honorary Secretary, Maurice Earley, on an outing at Saunderton on the Great Western Railway in the summer of 1937. Smartly dressed for the occasion, they are, from left to right, G. Lander, H. C. Doyle, G. R. Grigs, H. Gordon Tidey, E. R. Wethersett and C. R. L. Coles. They are all equipped with folding glass plate cameras.

Earley P1

A 4-2-2 locomotive heads the 'Zulu', the Great Western Railway's
3pm train from London Paddington to Plymouth, on the broad gauge
tracks through Ealing in 1890. The service, which averaged 53mph
for the 226-mile journey, was the fastest in Britain in its day and an
obvious attraction for Tice F. Budden, who was enthralled by speed.
Picturing the train from head-on made it easier to arrest the motion
using the slow photographic emulsions of the day.

LGRP 21601

One of William Dean's elegant 4-2-2 locomotives of the Great
Western Railway, No.3050 *Royal Sovereign* caught at speed leaving
Box Tunnel on 23rd September 1898 with the 7.15am express from
Falmouth to London Paddington. With their 7ft 8in driving wheels
and polished brass and copper fittings, the Dean 'Singles' epitomised
GWR express steam at the turn of the century, but all had been
withdrawn by the end of 1915.

GWR T1/15

On 12th August 1899 an official photographer superbly captured Great Western Railway No.3030 *Westward Ho* living up to its name as it sped to the west near Bath at the head of the 10.30am from Paddington to Falmouth.

GWR TI/13

In the summer of 1904, before the housing and commercial development spreading out of London had consumed the green fields, Great Western Railway '36xx' class 2-4-2T locomotive No.3611 heads a suburban express through Acton.

LGRP 21405 (Budden)

An outstanding example of early 'action' photography: a moving express caught in full flight by P. W. Pilcher. A London & North Western Railway train from London Euston to Liverpool is passing over Whitmore water troughs, between Stafford and Crewe, on 13th September 1905. The locomotives, a pair of 'Precedent' class 2-4-0s Nos.2180 *Perseverance* and 2001 *Henry Crosfield*, are picking up water by means of scoops lowered under their tenders. The leading locomotive's tank is full and water is cascading over the other engine, which will now be dipping its scoop in turn.

Water troughs, enabling locomotives to replenish their water supplies on the move, were an important factor in increasing the distances which could be worked without stopping.

Burtt 6247

Another of Pilcher's fine action shots captures London & North
Western Railway three-cylinder 2-2-2-0 compound No.1305 *Doric*
heading away from Shrewsbury past Bayston Hill with the 10.45am
stopping train to Cardiff on 26th May 1905. The line between
Shrewsbury and Hereford was jointly owned by the LNWR and the
Great Western Railway. The train is made up of GWR carriages and
some LNWR six-wheel stock.

FB 6185

The London, Tilbury & Southend Railway was a small but busy railway whose title largely defined its territory. For its passenger traffic it relied on a fleet of 4-4-2 tank locomotives which were named after places on or around its system. No.40 *Black Horse Road* is accelerating away from Southend for Fenchurch Street in about 1903.

LGRP 21457   (Budden)

The Somerset & Dorset Joint Railway had a main line from Bath to a junction near Bournemouth and branches to Wells, Bridgwater and Burnham. Its rural setting and its severe gradients over the Mendips made it a favourite with enthusiasts and photographers right up to its closure in 1966. During the summer, heavy through trains from the North and Midlands transported holidaymakers to the south coast. However, for most of the year lightly-loaded local services met passenger needs as epitomised by this train hauled by 4-4-0 locomotive No. 14 near Blandford in about 1895.

LGRP 21151   (Budden)

A fine panned action shot by E. R. Wethersett of the first London, Midland & Scottish Railway 4-6-2 locomotive No.6200 *The Princess Royal* speeding the 5.30pm Euston to Liverpool express through Hatch End on 5th July 1941. Despite nearly two years of wartime stringency No.6200 is still in presentable condition and in fact, although many locomotives received a plain black 'austerity' livery during the war years, the 'Princess Royal' class retained the LMS crimson lake throughout. Clues to the wartime period, however, are the blacked-out cab window and the sheeting between cab roof and tender, both intended to reduce glare from the firebox at night. Few enthusiasts were able to photograph railways during the Second World War, because of security controls and the shortage of film.

LPC 24366

Tom Williams' railway photographs were mostly produced in the West Country and the Midlands, but this view of the British Railways 'Britannia' class 4-6-2 locomotive *Thomas Hardy* was taken at Shap in Cumberland on 25th July 1964. Williams often experimented with 'panning', following the speeding train with his camera to blur the background to create an enhanced impression of movement.

Williams 9964

Speed powerfully conveyed by a low viewpoint, a wide angled lens and a long exposure in this image from the British Transport Films 1967 production *Rail* showing an electric locomotive on the West Coast route to Scotland.

BTF 10393

This, to modern eyes, rather curiously manipulated photograph, was
produced to advertise the London & North Western Railway's
American Special train service, which carried Transatlantic steamer
passengers from Liverpool's Riverside Station to London Euston.
Produced in 1909, it was a composite of photographs of the
carriages, station, staff and passengers with additional figures drawn
by a graphic artist. Screen printed in an advertising brochure, this
image would probably not have appeared as crude as this
reproduction.

LMS 1859

An official photograph, publicising the London & North Western Railway's dining carriages and dating from about 1905. Photographs of carriages from this period rarely included the passengers. Using the cameras and plates of the day, images such as this would have been virtually impossible to take on a moving train, because of the long exposure required in the rather dimly-lit carriage.

LMS 355

The centenary of the Liverpool & Manchester Railway was celebrated by an exhibition and pageant staged in Liverpool in September 1930. Historical transport was shown in a series of tableaux. Episode One portrayed a caveman dragging his bride home by her hair, closely observed by what was described as a dragon. The cave man was played by Cecil Mason, the cave woman by Paddie O'Hara and the front half of the dragon by E. W. Lawson. The programme did not credit the back legs.

Derby 16758

The 'Flying Scotsman', the 10.00am departure from London King's Cross to Edinburgh, is arguably the world's most famous express passenger service. When the London & North Eastern Railway introduced non-stop running in 1928 it commissioned the specialist architectural photographers Bedford Lemere to make a record of its fashionable carriages. The facilities included a restaurant, cocktail bar, ladies' retiring room and even a barber's, where male passengers could while away part of the $8\frac{1}{4}$-hour journey.

Doncaster 107L 29560

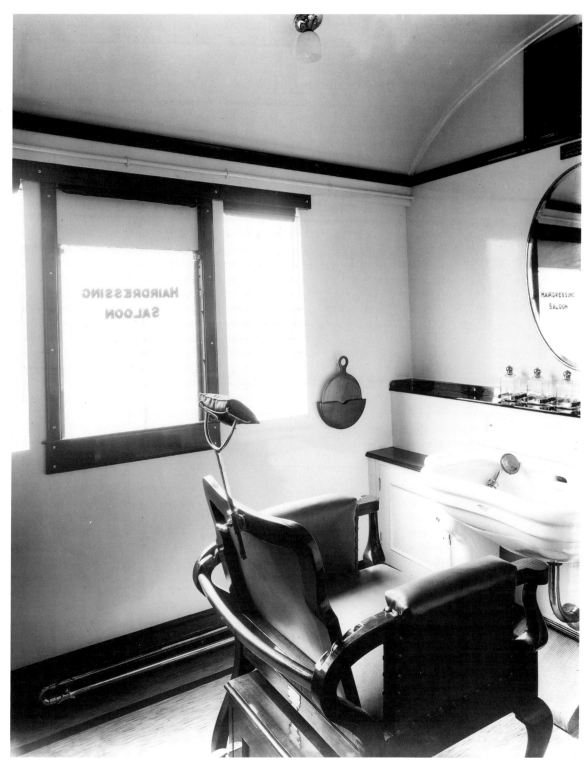

The interior of a Great Western Railway buffet car was photographed by Fox Films in September 1938 for the following year's *Holiday Haunts* brochure. The buffet car provided a new way of eating on trains, for passengers were no longer restricted to the formalities of the dining car as they ate and drank in the buffet before returning to their seats. It had a spacious counter at one end and tables at the other.

These images were elaborately posed with the carriage apparently passing through open country, but the background scenery has been added for effect and the photographs were probably taken in the Swindon works yard! Images from this shoot were widely used in the company's publicity material.

GWR B 13485

GWR B13491

Camping coaches, railway carriages converted to provide accommodation for six or eight people, were introduced by several railway companies from 1933. The relatively low rent, typically about £3 a week, made them immediately popular and soon each of the 'Big Four' railway companies offered camping holidays. By 1935 there were over 200 camping coaches located at 160 holiday destinations across the country. This is a Great Western Railway coach pictured by Fox Photographs in March 1936. The unseasonable date and the use of the same models as in many other GWR publicity shots suggests that it is a posed view.

GWR B12112

The buffet bar of one of the controversial tavern cars which appeared in 1949. The novel design originated on the Southern Railway before nationalisation. It was unlike anything seen before. Half the exterior was painted to resemble brickwork up to waistband level with pseudo-half timbering and stucco above. In one panel was a painted 'traditional' pub sign, in this case, 'At the Sign of the White Horse'. The interior was a mock 'olde-worlde' pub with artificial beams and lantern-style lamps. The other half of the vehicle, conventionally painted outside, contained a first class dining saloon. The tavern cars were converted to conventional buffets in 1959 and 1960 — to few people's regret, it would seem.

Clapham 195/8/64

Exhausted Belgian soldiers find it hard to smile for the Southern
Railway photographer as they wait to board a London-bound train at
Margate, following their evacuation from Dunkirk on 4 June 1940. In
the Second World War official railway photographers used skills they
had perfected in advertising and publicity work in propaganda
images.

Clapham 761/67

The 'Night Ferry' service, connecting with the cross-Channel sailings, was one of the best-known trains to run from London's Victoria station. Its sleeping cars and luggage vans were shipped from Dover across the Channel to Dunkirk, enabling the traveller to the Continent to retire to bed in London and emerge from the sheets in France. The 'Night Ferry' brought to Britain the distinctively European carriages of the Compagnie Internationale des Wagons-Lits. After a wartime break the 'Night Ferry' service resumed its nocturnal peregrinations and in 1957 it gained a through coach to Brussels.

'Battle of Britain' class 4-6-2 locomotive No.21C156 *Croydon* is depicted at the head of the first post-war 'Night Ferry' awaiting departure from Victoria on 15th December 1947. With the train routed over the more difficult Chatham route to Dover, *Croydon* has the assistance of a Maunsell L1 class 4-4-0 locomotive. Changing travel habits led to the withdrawal of the 'Night Ferry' service in 1980.

Clapham 30/68

The sixteenth century
Guildhall at Much Wenlock
in Shropshire, a Great
Western Railway publicity
photograph taken in
September 1923.

GWR B 3951

Weymouth, in Dorset, was a popular location for holidays and excursions, and the summer passenger traffic generated considerable revenue for the Great Western Railway. The resort regularly featured in the company's *Holiday Haunts* brochure. This view of the sands and Esplanade was taken by an official photographer in August 1929.

GWR B 8513

Lyme Regis in Dorset was served by a branch line from Axminster in Devon, which at the time this photograph was taken, in August 1936, was operated by the Southern Railway. Despite this, the resort regularly featured in the Great Western Railway's guide, *Holiday Haunts*, as it fell within the company's general sphere of influence and could be reached by connecting services from GWR stations. This photograph appeared in the 1939 brochure.

GWR B12400

Weymouth harbour in August 1929, pictured by a Great Western Railway photographer as one of Cosens paddle steamers returns from a pleasure cruise.

GWR B 8517

Fishing vessels in Mevagissey harbour in Cornwall in September 1928, a photograph by the Great Western Railway's publicity department. The nearest station, St. Austell, was some six miles away, but the village was served by a connecting bus service run by the GWR's subsidiary, Western National.

GWR B 7812

An animated scene at Holyhead station in 1909. Passengers wait to board a London express after disembarking from a tender which had ferried them from the SS *Cedric*. Meanwhile their luggage mounts up; a formidable selection of trunks indicates why separate luggage vans were an essential feature of important expresses, especially boat trains. Most are labelled to London but that might not be the end of their journeys: one trunk is inscribed 'Miss C. Wallace, Shanghai'.

LMS   1884

Keen to find new ways of attracting custom, the Caledonian Railway set up a semi-independent company in 1914 to build a hotel and golf course at Gleneagles on its main line to Perth. The outbreak of the First World War delayed construction, so when this photograph of the 18th tee on the Queen's Course was taken in 1923, the hotel was only just nearing completion.

Gleneagles 146

British Transport Films crews ranged far beyond road and railways in their coverage, touching on subjects which had only the most tangential connections with road and rail. *Modern Architecture* was a filmstrip produced in 1954 and featured these blocks of flats in Page Street, Westminster, designed by Sir Edwin Lutyens. The accompanying lecture notes remarked that, despite the steel framework, these were buildings in the Georgian Classical style.

BTF 2422

Publicity photographs usually emphasised the pleasures of rail travel, posing models in glamorous settings in the best appointed carriages. The British Transport Films photographers adopted a more naturalistic style, evident in this image taken during the making of '*Party Travel*' in 1950. The documentary advertised British Railways' group bookings services by following a works outing from Leicester to London.

BTF 424

Some of the British Transport Films cameramen and directors went on to work on the 'kitchen sink' dramas of the 1960s. However, this image, from the 1954 production *A Day of One's Own*, was intended to show a 'typical' housewife completing her laundry before taking the train for a relaxing day out.

BTF 2687

British Railways 'West Country' class locomotive No.34016 *Bodmin*
heads across the River Taw towards Barnstaple Town station in 1953.
The Southern Region was best known for its complex network of
lines south of London and for its main lines to the south coast and
Kent, but it also extended deep into Devon and Cornwall. Its West of
England services, including the 'Atlantic Coast Express' shown here,
connected many favourite holiday resorts with London. The lengthy
train which had left Waterloo in the morning would, by mid-
afternoon, have separated into up to seven sections wandering the
branches to such destinations as Padstow, Exmouth and Bude.
Barnstaple was served by through coaches detached at Exeter Central
which continued on to Ilfracombe after shedding a carriage for
Torrington at Barnstaple Junction.

BTF 1855

One of the most dramatic lines in Britain is the West Highland line
from Glasgow over the wilds of Rannoch Moor to the foothills of Ben
Nevis at Fort William. Amongst many memorable features of the
route is the 'Horseshoe Curve' between Tyndrum and Bridge of
Orchy where the cash-starved railway company, rather than face the
expense of a long viaduct to pursue a direct course, took its line
around the flanks of Ben Odhar, Ben a Chaistel and Ben Doran with
viaducts to carry it across the two intervening glens. A pair of LNER
K2 2-6-0 locomotives is heading a heavy train from Fort William to
Glasgow during the mid-1950s.

BTF 1446

Prison warders escort convicts to their train at London's Waterloo Station in August 1960, in a scene from John Schlesinger's award-winning British Transport Films documentary *Terminus*. The film, accompanied by music but no commentary, depicted a day in the life of London's busiest station and was seen by over five million people.

BTF 4766

An 0-6-2T locomotive with a train of mineral wagons crosses Crumlin Viaduct — one of the most impressive railway structures in South Wales — on 24th March 1963. Completed in 1855, this cast and wrought iron viaduct spanned the Ebbw Valley in Monmouthshire; its total length was 1,658ft and its height 200ft.

Linfoot   3/104A

A dramatic action shot of 4-6-0 locomotive No.7005 *Lamphey Castle*, caught by a shaft of sunlight against a glowering sky, at Kingham on the Oxford to Worcester line on 3rd November 1962.

Linfoot   4/142A

Linfoot   5/162 B

The short branch between Havant and Hayling Island in Hampshire was worked for much of its existence by diminutive 'Terrier' tank locomotives. They were ideally suited to it, because of the weight restrictions on the timber viaduct across the Langstone Channel. Locomotive No.32678 (right), south of Havant station, is dwarfed by its carriages. The ageing rolling stock and the condition of Langstone Bridge were important factors in the decision to close the branch in 1963; this view of the sunset over Langstone Harbour (above) was taken on 2nd November, the last day of services.

M. D. England

A 'Castle' class 4-6-0 locomotive at the head of a local service near Brimscombe Crossing in Gloucestershire on 14th May 1961. Linfoot chose a vantage point that set the train in the landscape, but a photographer visible at lineside is taking a typical 'threequarters' view.

Linfoot   2/107 B

The Brecon & Merthyr line was one of the most scenic branches in South Wales but the sparsely-populated area through which it passed was a significant factor in its closure at the end of 1962. On 29th December, the last day of the service between Brecon and Newport, Tom Linfoot set out in the snow to record '57xx' class 0-6-0PT locomotive No.4679 leaving Pentir Rhiw, the wisps of steam from under the carriages indicating that the steam heating is keeping the passengers warm.

Linfoot   4/153 B

A British Railways Standard Class 5 4-6-0 locomotive passes with a Ramsgate train. The Southern Region of British Railways inherited a considerable mileage of electrified track and at the end of the 1950s embarked on a major programme to extend electrification through Kent. Work on the Kent Coast scheme is well in hand in this view, with the third rail already in place.

Click

A begrimed 'Battle of Britain' 4-6-2 locomotive No.34067 *Tangmere* heads a Dover express near Bromley South in about 1960. Most of the vehicles are in the green livery which the British Railways Southern Region adopted in the late 1950s but several are still in the earlier crimson and cream colour scheme, familiarly referred to as "blood and custard"!

Click   4/130

Winter on the West Highland line. Against a backdrop of the conical peak of Ben Doran, a Class 27 diesel-electric locomotive heads a Fort William-Glasgow train towards the County March summit, north of Tyndrum in about 1970. Treacy chose a virtually identical vantage point to Cyril Herbert, who pictured a K2 class locomotive passing this spot with a passenger train in September 1952 (see page 119).

Treacy   EC 9

The Snowdon Mountain Railway, running from Llanberis, at 353ft above sea level, to the summit 3,493ft above sea level, is Britain's only rack railway and includes gradients as steep as 1 in 5.5. Locomotive No.6 Padarn is seen below Clogwyn station, at a level of around 2,550ft. The locomotive propels the carriage up the mountain and the descent is by gravity, with the carriage 'checked' by the engine; the two are never coupled.

Ransome-Wallis

A Class 81 electric locomotive heads a freight train between Shap and Penrith on the West Coast main line. The photographer, Eric Treacy, never really took to colour film or modern traction, preferring to photograph steam locomotives in black and white, but the cloud formation and attractive landscape setting make this an ideal colour subject.

Treacy EC 26

A U2 class 4-4-0 locomotive, built by Beyer Peacock in 1948 for the Great Northern Railway of Ireland, passes Narrowater in County Down with a passenger train on 11 August 1963.

Linfoot 5/96B

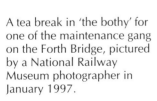

Wakefield Europort, seen here under construction in June 1995, was built to exploit the direct rail link to the Channel Tunnel and is the departure point for freight services from the north of England to the Continent.

NRM   LT 950418

A tea break in 'the bothy' for one of the maintenance gang on the Forth Bridge, pictured by a National Railway Museum photographer in January 1997.

NRM   LT 7970734

Charing Cross station, as seen by a National Railway Museum photographer on its reopening in November 1990 following a major reconstruction project.

NRM   LT 930379

A Class 156 diesel passing Badicaul on the Inverness to Kyle of Lochalsh line in the summer of 1997. The photograph was taken by the National Railway Museum photographer, Chris Hogg, as part of a joint project with Railtrack Scotland to commemorate the centenary of the line.

NRM   LT 970813

Documenting developments on the contemporary railway is a major component of the work of the National Railway Museum's photographers and in 1989 this included recording the electrification of the East Coast Main Line between London and Scotland. These workers on the roof of the electrification train are tying off the catenary wires on the overhead power lines.

NRM 311/89

Recording the construction of the Channel Tunnel was one of the largest projects undertaken by the National Railway Museum photographers. Here the Marine Running Tunnel (South) Boring Machine is making its way across the UK crossover towards France in September 1990. On the right is the narrow gauge line used by the contractors trains which removed the spoil.

NRM 1110/90

Contractors on the roof of the £130 million Waterloo International Terminal, departure point for the cross-Channel Eurostar service, during its construction in September 1991.

NRM 726/91

The London & South Western Railway Servants' Orphanage at Woking was opened in July 1909 to care for the children of railway workers who died in service. Shortly before its closure in 1988 it was the subject of a special study by the National Railway Museum's photographers.

NRM 455/88

In 1980 the National Railway Museum's South Eastern & Chatham
Railway 'Wainwright D' 4-4-0 locomotive No.737 was used for a
scene in the film *Chariots of Fire*, about the 1924 Olympic Games.
Ben Cross, playing the athlete Harold Abrahams, greets Cheryl
Campbell on the platform at York station, amidst artificially-generated
steam.

NRM 590/80

Part Two

AT THE
LINESIDE

Godfrey Soole captures a
fellow photographer
recording GWR '43xx' 2-6-0
locomotive No. 4386
crossing the Stapleton Road
bridge on the descent into
Bristol from the South Wales
main line at the head of an
express freight. Behind the
photographer the 'T' board
indicates the termination of
temporary speed restriction.
GWR locomotives continued
to maintain a right-hand
driving position and the
signal post is positioned on
the side of the track where
the driver will have the best
sight of it.

Soole   806

'Jubilee' class 4-6-0 locomotive No.45567 *South Australia* climbs out of Liverpool Lime Street station through the Edge Hill cuttings in the mid-1950s. The photographer, Eric Treacy, had been a vicar in Liverpool, where he learnt the best times to take photographs at Edge Hill: the brief periods each day when shafts of sunlight penetrated to the bottom of the cuttings. He also befriended many of the footplate crews who worked on the line, occasionally persuading them to create special smoke effects for the camera.

Treacy LS-F-3003

The Cambrian Railways, with a main line from Oswestry to Aberystwyth and the coast line to Barmouth and Pwllheli, was one of the Welsh companies which were grouped into the Great Western in 1923. 2-4-0 locomotive No.28 was photographed by T. F. Budden at Barmouth with a northbound train of six-wheeled carriages in about 1900.

LGRP 21250

What many regard as the zenith of Great Western steam: 'King' class 4-6-0 locomotive No.6023 *King Edward II* heading its most famous train, the 'Cornish Riviera Limited', on the Westbury cut-off in about 1936. The cut-off, a stretch of line built to avoid the congested junctions around Westbury station, was completed in 1933 with the aid of funds provided at low interest under a Government scheme devised to alleviate unemployment.

Soole 1561

An early experiment in alternative motive power was the steam turbine condensing locomotive. Examples were tried in various overseas countries during the last decade of the nineteenth century but the first in Britain was the Reid-Ramsay locomotive built at the North British Locomotive Company's works in Glasgow in 1910. Current was supplied by a generator driven by a steam turbine to four traction motors, the machine being known as the 'Electric-Turbo-Loco'. It was tested on the lines of the North British and Caledonian Railways around Glasgow, but without success. This Caledonian Railway official photograph shows the condenser end of the locomotive shortly after its completion, locomotive and photographer attracting the attention of some uncompromising-looking young Glaswegians.

St Rollox 371

An exceptional scene on the Lickey Incline near Bromsgrove, recorded in two photographs taken by Dr. Pat Ransome-Wallis. The Incline, over two miles long and with a gradient of 1 in 37.7, is the steepest continuous section of track on any of Britain's main lines. Spending a day recording traffic on the line in March 1950, Ransome-Wallis was surprised to see a 42-wagon freight train hauled by the Garratt locomotive No.47972, which had been built for the London, Midland & Scottish Railway. It was assisted by the local 'banker', locomotive No.69999, another Garratt which had once served the London & North Eastern Railway. The Garratts, with their twin sets of independent driving wheels, cylinders and motions mounted on separate chassis, were rare enough sights on their own, so Ransome-Wallis and his companion drove flat out to get in position to photograph them together. Their haste proved unnecessary, for both locomotives stalled and they had to be rescued by the 0-10-0 banking engine, nicknamed 'Big Bertha'. Ransome-Wallis, no fan of nationalisation, commented "What a sight — but oh, my income tax!".

Ransome-Wallis 7818

Ransome-Wallis 8587

The construction of two large masonry dams in Upper Nidderdale, in the West Riding of Yorkshire, to impound water supplies for the city of Bradford, was a major undertaking during the early years of the twentieth century. These remote yet imposing structures located at Angram and Scar House, were completed in 1919 and 1936 respectively. Railways were an essential feature of most major construction projects and Household's photograph shows the temporary track laid during the construction of the second dam in the early summer of 1928. The large stone blocks were cut from the adjacent hillside. The locomotive is a Hudswell Clarke 0-4-0ST *Craven* supplied to Bradford Corporation by the Leeds builders in early 1920.
Household 537

The Class 55 'Deltic' diesel locomotive No.9003 *Meld* leaves Leeds Central station with a southbound passenger train in the early 1960s. The photographer, Bishop Eric Treacy, was often allowed special access to areas denied to many railway photographers and composed this shot through the signal box doorway.

Treacy 35/1/11

Arrivals at London's King's Cross station in the late 1950s, seen through the distinctive brick arches of Lewis Cubitt's 1852 train shed. The locomotives at Platforms 6 and 7 are Class A3 No.60112 *St. Simon* and Class B1 No.61374.

Herbert R60/8/6

'Steam up and waiting', Cyril Herbert's view of London & North Eastern Railway B1 class locomotives at York shed on 11th August 1947.

Herbert R24 31

Bishop Eric Treacy frequently visited the picturesque Lune Valley, where in the mid-1950s he took this photograph of British Railways Class 5 4-6-0 locomotive No 45435 heading south with a passenger express train. Artists and photographers soon came to view railways as an accepted part of the landscape.

Treacy   LS-F-2187A

In its closing years the Great Western Railway ordered two experimental gas turbine locomotives for express passenger work, one from Metropolitan-Vickers of Manchester, the other from the Swiss manufacturer Brown, Boveri. They were delivered in 1949, after nationalisation. On the Western Region of British Railways they undertook a considerable amount of running on test trains and regular services. Although the performance of the locomotives showed promise, the gas turbine principle was not ultimately adopted. Standing at Bristol Temple Meads station on 31st May 1952, the Metro-Vic locomotive No.18100 attracts the curiosity of 'platform-enders' after hauling the 11.15am 'Merchant Venturer' train from Paddington.

Williams 1489

Cyril Herbert titled this shot of a Norwegian State Railways *Kriegslok* 'Wet Night In Trondheim'. On holiday in Norway in September 1953, Herbert was attracted to his subject by the motion inspection lights, which were left on whilst the locomotive was running. Resting his Leica camera on a porter's barrow, Herbert guessed at the composition because he could not use the viewfinder and allowed an exposure of over 40 seconds to compensate for the failing light. The resulting print was circulated, to critical acclaim, amongst fellow members of the Railway Photographic Society.

Herbert R51 C6 23

'West Country' class locomotive No.34017 *Ilfracombe* meanders through the rolling Devon countryside near Tavistock with a westbound train of modest proportions on 14th April 1951. Although designed for heavy passenger services, the axle loading of these engines made them suitable for the lightly-engineered West of England branches.

Russell-Smith 395

The shadows lengthen as the late summer sun catches locomotive No.6025 *King Henry III* as it leaves Kennoway Tunnel and runs along the sea wall at Dawlish with a London-bound express in 1955. It attracts only a casual glance from a couple strolling with a large dog but interrupts the view of a lady gazing out to sea. The age of the private motorist is fast coming, as the latest styles of the 1950s mingle with pre-war models in the car park.

Ransome-Wallis 10943

This Tom Williams' photograph taken in June 1973 makes an interesting comparison with Dr. Pat Ransome-Wallis' view at roughly the same location eighteen years earlier. Steam traction has given way to diesel-hydraulic with locomotive No. D1069 *Western Vanguard* running on to the sea wall at Dawlish.

Williams 10252

A spectacular setting from an interesting vantage point: the Bristol to Portishead branch where the Avon Gorge is spanned by the famous Clifton Suspension Bridge. The line was opened in 1867 and was on the broad gauge until it was converted to standard gauge in 1880. Running bunker first, a GWR '45xx' class 2-6-2T locomotive is emerging from Clifton Bridge No.2 Tunnel with a local for Portishead in about 1934. The passenger service on the branch was withdrawn in 1964.

Soole 270

Leslie Overend, who made his career in journalism and photography, was a lifelong locomotive enthusiast. The railways' mark on the landscape is clearly shown in his photograph of Class 5 4-6-0 locomotive No 45368 crossing Capenwray Viaduct near Carnforth in Lancashire on the old Furness & Midland Joint line.

Overend 123

British Railways 2P class 4-4-0 locomotive No.40569, built for the London, Midland & Scottish Railway, entering Templecombe with a train from Bath on the Somerset & Dorset line, 6th June 1949. The Somerset & Dorset Joint Railway had been formed in the 1860s to provide a route from the Midlands and the North to the new resort of Bournemouth on the south coast. The line, which was closed by 1966, passed through some of the most picturesque parts of the West Country and was always popular with railway photographers.

Henton (S&D)

John Click chose a low viewpoint to emphasise the sweep of the tracks when he photographed this Southern Region train, made up of four-car electric units, in the early 1960s.

Click S 297

The triple-heading of trains was an exceptional practice but was often used for working heavy boat trains up the 1 in 36 gradient from Folkestone Harbour to Folkestone Junction. The sharp change of gradient is noticeable around the middle of the train. This photograph was taken by E. R. Wethersett in about 1949.

LPC 23163

'West Country' class locomotive No.34092 *City of Wells* speeds along an embankment with the 'Golden Arrow' Pullman boat train. The prestigious 'Golden Arrow' service connected London's Victoria station with the Channel ports and ferries to the Continent.

Click S 102

4-6-0 locomotive No.7918
Rhose Wood Hall passes
over Evesham Road level
crossing on its way out of
Stratford-upon-Avon in May
1964. The new signal box
was opened in 1960 to
replace two existing boxes
and work a new connection
over which ironstone was
routed from Banbury to
South Wales.

Williams 9870

Western Region motive
power meets in Harbury
cutting, near Leamington
Spa, in the summer of 1962
on one of those fortuitous
occasions which enable a
photographer to record two
trains passing. Nos.5008
Raglan Castle and 6001 *King
Edward VII* are the
locomotives.

Williams 9243

The country branch line is typified by this delightful photograph of a
Neath to Brecon train wandering through the countryside near
Sennybridge in the spring sunshine in May 1952, headed by a Great
Western Railway '57xx' class pannier tank locomotive No.3767. At
one time nowhere in England and Wales was much more than
twenty miles from at least a wayside halt, but declining passenger
numbers meant that in the 1960s many branch lines disappeared,
victims of what became known as the 'Beeching Axe'. The last Neath
to Brecon train passed this way in 1962, even before publication of
the 'Beeching Report'.

It was the idyllic setting of the slumbering stations with their well-
tended gardens which attracted railway photographers. J. R. Russell-
Smith, who produced this image, admitted that he worked "primarily
for the excitement of photographing moving trains. . . . For my own
enjoyment they were mostly taken in pleasant rural settings".

Russell-Smith 513

Like the local passenger train, the pick-up goods train was another feature of the branch line. It made slow progress, calling at the station depots and sidings along its route, shunting the yards as required and setting down and collecting wagons. Freight traffic handled in slow, loose-coupled unbraked vehicles in trains made up of single wagonloads proved vulnerable to road competition. By the 1960s the railway regarded wagon-load traffic as uneconomic and it disappeared in favour of 'block' freight trains carrying a single commodity direct between terminals. "Emmet-like trains going clanketty-clank through our countryside" was how the chairman of the British Transport Commission had described loose-coupled freights such as this local pick-up headed by 'Dean Goods' 0-6-0 locomotive No.2538, photographed near Rhayader on the mid-Wales line on 9th October 1950.

Russell-Smith 371

North and mid Wales were notable for the many narrow gauge railways serving the local industries — principally slate — in the mountainous areas where standard gauge lines would be too costly to build. The Corris Railway was opened in 1859 to a gauge of 2ft 3ins as a horse-worked line between Machynlleth and the quarries at Corris and Aberllefenni, in the foothills of Cader Idris. Locomotives were introduced in 1878. The atmosphere of the Welsh narrow gauge slate railway is admirably summed up by this view of a train of empty wagons snaking between the houses at Corris on their way back up to the quarries on 8th January 1943, five years before the line closed. The photographer was Selwyn Pearce-Higgins who specialised in recording the minor railways.

Pearce-Higgins COR/24

A line with a quite different character was the narrow gauge
Welshpool & Llanfair Light Railway, opened in 1903 and worked by
the Cambrian Railways. Constructed to a gauge of 2ft 6in, the
W&LLR ran through the Banwy Valley where it served a
predominantly agricultural area. Although it lost its passenger traffic
under Great Western ownership in 1931, it continued to provide a
local goods service until as late as 1956 when it was closed by
British Railways. 0-6-0T locomotive No.822 was photographed by
Selwyn Pearce-Higgins in the woods between Cyfronydd and
Heniarth during an 'informal' stop for the benefit of a local resident.
The Welshpool & Llanfair was re-opened by a preservation society in
1963.

NRM 57/91

Thomas Scotton combined his love of landscape and railways in this
photograph of Midland Railway '1070 class' 2-4-0 locomotive
No.142 hauling an express train through Ashwood Dale near Buxton
on 19th June 1912. The photograph was intended for use as a
carriage print.

Derby 9786

In the open countryside of East Anglia, an ex-Great Eastern Railway
Class F4 2-4-2T locomotive threads through an agricultural
landscape near Trumpington with a train from Cambridge to
Haverhill on 31st July 1934. Most of the accommodation is six-wheel
stock of some vintage but the first two vehicles are horse boxes.
There are also vans, probably for fresh fruit and vegetables which
will be worked on to London for sale at the Covent Garden markets.

LPC 24794 (Wethersett)

Descending the rope-worked 1 in 13 Pwllyrhebog Incline on the
former Taff Vale Railway branch from Tonypandy to the Clydach Vale
Colliery in the Rhondda Valley. The incline, three-quarters of a mile
in length, was operated by a stationary engine which drove two inter-
geared drums, so that a descending train counterbalanced an
ascending one. In 1949 Dr. Patrick Ransome-Wallis traversed the
incline on the footplate of 0-6-0T locomotive No.194, one of three
specially constructed for use on the line. A feature of the design was
the coned boiler which prevented the water level falling below the
top of the firebox whilst on the gradient. From the cab window,
Ransome-Wallis recorded a scene which shows No.193 making the
balancing ascent against a backdrop of grey colliery terraces and
chapels.

Ransome-Wallis 11014

The railway in the landscape: Sugar Loaf Mountain near Abergavenny in Monmouthshire, seen from the footplate of the northbound British Railways Class 4 4-6-0 locomotive No 75007 in 1952.

Ransome-Wallis 9535

The textile mills of the West Riding of Yorkshire were still in full production on 7th September 1945 when LMS 4F 0-6-0 No.4128 was photographed by E. R. Wethersett passing over the water troughs at Luddendenfoot, near Sowerby Bridge, with a train of coal empties returning to the south Yorkshire pits. The Calder Valley line of the Manchester & Leeds Railway (later the Lancashire & Yorkshire) was the first of the trans-Pennine routes, engineered by George Stephenson and completed in 1841. The railway played a major part in shaping the industrial landscape pictured here.

LPC 24465

A train of coal empties heads back north out of London behind a former London & North Western Railway '19in Goods' 4-6-0 locomotive No.8824, passing Hatch End on 31st March 1934. The wooden-bodied coal wagons would not be fitted with automatic brakes so the train would make a fairly leisurely progress, not exceeding the 35mph maximum generally prescribed for unfitted freight trains. The residents of the desirable 'semis' of the outer London suburbs would probably be somewhat less enthralled than the photographer, E. R. Wethersett, by volcanic displays of exhaust such as this. They would be much more appreciative of the electric trains which ran on the adjacent tracks out to Watford.

LPC 24399

Electric powered trains were, for most railway photographers, a poor
substitute for steam, but Ransome-Wallis produced images of some of
the most prosaic vehicles. The Kent Coast Express, made up of three
four-car electric units, also attracted the interest of a group of boys as
it passed near Faversham in 1959.

Ransome-Wallis 11861

British Railways Class 2
2-6-2T locomotive
No.44028 passing Grove
Ferry on the Canterbury to
Ramsgate line in 1956, as a
family outing crosses the
River Stour on the hand-
hauled ferry.

Ransome-Wallis 9510

One of the classic locations favoured by so many railway photographers, including Maurice Earley: Dillicar water troughs in the wild solitude of the Lune Valley on the West Coast Main Line. London, Midland & Scottish 'Princess Royal' class locomotive No.6203 *Princess Margaret Rose* replenishes its water tank after tackling the climb to Shap Summit with the southbound 'Mid-day Scot' on 29th July 1936.

Earley 5403

Maurice Earley did not confine himself to standard threequarter views and stood back from the line at Shap to photograph No.6222 *Queen Mary* with the London, Midland & Scottish Railway's prestigious 'Coronation Scot' streamlined service from London to Glasgow on 24th July 1939. It was harder to 'freeze' movement in a profile view, so Earley set the shutter speed at 1/800.

Earley 10/8

Class 5 4-6-0 locomotive No.45133 heads north through the Lune Gorge, passing over Dillicar water troughs, with a train of banana vans in the mid-1950s. The legend 'Steam-Bananas' shows that the vans are steam heated to aid ripening during transit.

Treacy LS-2012F

The change from steam to diesel traction on British Railways proved difficult and locomotive failures were not uncommon. On 25th July 1964, Tom Williams was photographing on the climb to Shap Summit when a Class 40 diesel-electric locomotive broke down. A 2-6-4T steam banking engine and another Class 40 diesel with a following train were brought up to the rear of the 'crippled' train to propel it away.

Williams 9968

A railway which has been relatively little photographed is the
Cheshire Lines Committee route between Chester, Northwich and
Altrincham but J. F. Russell-Smith took a number of photographs
there shortly after nationalisation in 1948. On 26th February he was
well placed on an overbridge to record 0-6-0 locomotive No.5194
heading away on a local passenger train near Knutsford, its exposed
cab revealing a footplate crew somewhat bemused to find themselves
being photographed.

Russell-Smith 79

Lincoln in 1950, as Class B1 4-6-0 locomotive No.61248 eases over
the Pelham Street level crossing into Central station with the signal
gantry directing it onto the left-most track. Road traffic is still sparse
but anyone who had a model railway layout in the '50s will have
placed on it a 'Matchbox' version of everything shown here!

Williams 11266

Class A4 4-6-2 locomotive No.60003 *Andrew K. McCosh* crosses the border between England and Scotland north of Berwick with the 'Capitals Limited' non-stop from London King's Cross to Edinburgh, in this photograph taken by E. R. Wethersett on 12th August 1950. The ingenious corridor tender allowed a relief footplate crew to take over at the halfway point on the journey. The non-stop service remained the highlight of the summer timetable until 1962, its 392½-mile journey being the longest regular steam-worked service in the world.

LPC 23990

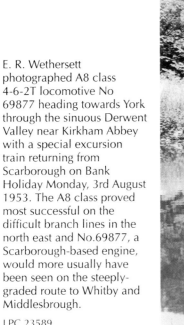

E. R. Wethersett photographed A8 class 4-6-2T locomotive No 69877 heading towards York through the sinuous Derwent Valley near Kirkham Abbey with a special excursion train returning from Scarborough on Bank Holiday Monday, 3rd August 1953. The A8 class proved most successful on the difficult branch lines in the north east and No.69877, a Scarborough-based engine, would more usually have been seen on the steeply-graded route to Whitby and Middlesbrough.

LPC 23589

The most dedicated railway photographers often travelled great
distances to picture locomotives in attractive settings and Cyril
Herbert regularly visited Scotland to capture locomotives amidst
appropriate scenery. In this September 1952 view of a K2 2-6-0
locomotive on the West Highland line between Tyndrum and Bridge
of Orchy the approaching train draws the eye towards the romantic
landscape around Ben Doran.

NRM 170/97

Part Three

STATIONS AND STRUCTURES

An official photograph of the Midland Railway's Matlock Bath station in Derbyshire's Peak District in July 1889. It is probably the work of the elder Thomas Scotton. The railways had been largely responsible for the growth of Matlock Bath as a spa town, following the opening of the station in 1849.

Derby 3135

Wrought iron columns support the grandiose sweep of the roof at
Paddington station, photographed by Maurice Earley in 1952, nearly
one hundred years after the construction of Digby Wyatt's London
terminus for the Great Western Railway. Earley was one of only a
small group of railway photographers who took an interest in station
buildings, but he has also managed to record locomotive No.5018 *St.
Mawes Castle*, ready to depart with a Cheltenham train.

Earley 109/52

The Great Western Hotel at Paddington was opened in 1854, six months after the railway station, and was regarded as one of the finest hotels in London. A particular pride of the hotel was the coffee room described in 1860 as "divided by columns imitative of Sienna marble, with white capitals, above which is an order of terminal figures, and a deeply coffered ceiling, with coloured mouldings". In this view on 9th June 1922 it is functioning as a tea room, the tables laid with crisp linen and place settings, the obligatory potted palms defining the tone and the general ambience recalling the days when 'taking tea' was a more leisurely affair.

GWR B3776

Paddington station escaped the worst of the London Blitz until hit by incendiary bombs in January 1941, but the worst single incident was early on 17th April 1941 when a land mine exploded in the departure roadway. The main buildings were badly damaged and the boardroom and some offices demolished. Eighteen people were killed, but despite the devastation the station was quickly back in business and only a few early trains were cancelled. Great Western Railway publicity photographers were based at Paddington and they were on hand to record the incident — much of their output from the Second World War years documents the destruction caused by air raids.

GWR B Box 361/6

Cannon Street station was built on a bank of the Thames to serve London's commuter traffic from Kent and was approached by a bridge across the river. John Click, who worked for British Railways, was in a privileged position at trackside when he photographed a four-car suburban electric train departing, as the 'West Country' class locomotive *Barnstaple* waited at its platform. The delicately-arched roof had been badly damaged in an air raid in 1941, and was demolished in 1958, shortly after this photograph was taken.

Click 5/15

Passengers blurred by a long exposure setting pass through the ticket barriers at the Great Eastern Railway's Liverpool Street station on 2nd June 1920. The GER served the populous areas of the East End and its encouragement of suburban traffic with frequent trains and cheap fares led to many workers moving out of London to the outlying districts. Eventually Liverpool Street was to see the most intensively-worked steam-hauled suburban service in the world, the famous 'Jazz' service. This volume of activity gave the station a reputation for its sulphurous atmosphere, but full suburban electrification in 1960 finally dispelled Liverpool Street's worst murkiness.

Liverpool Street E 152

St. Pancras station in London's Euston Road, an official London,
Midland & Scottish Railway photograph dating from 1927. With its
elegant train shed designed by William Barlow and the magnificent
frontage of Sir Giles Gilbert Scott's Midland Grand Hotel, St. Pancras
was the most ornate of London's termini. The hotel, however, proved
difficult to adapt to the needs of the twentieth century and was
converted to offices eight years after this photograph was taken.

LMS 4549

One of the really great British railway stations was the old Euston, London's first main line terminus. Opened in 1837, it grew untidily but nevertheless included two of the finest symbols of the triumph of the new railway age, Philip Hardwick's Doric portico built in 1838 and his son Philip Charles Hardwick's Great Hall of 1849. Seen here in 1919, the portico stood 72ft high, a statement of the London & Birmingham Railway's confidence in its achievement and in the future.

LMS 3407

A new Euston was needed for the electrification of the West Coast Main Line to Manchester and Liverpool and the Great Hall was, amidst public protest, demolished. As the demolition men moved in, George Stephenson moved out, feet first, and now surveys the scene in another, though very different, Great Hall at the National Railway Museum.

Euston DM 7031

The demolition of the Doric portico at Euston station in 1961. The campaign against the destruction of the arch became something of a *cause celèbre* and many protesters argued that it should have been dismantled and re-erected on another site. The loss of the portico was a major influence in changing attitudes to the preservation of Britain's architectural heritage.

Euston   DM 4998

Euston   DM 8590

A Midland Railway 4-4-0 locomotive No.1021 heads an express from Manchester to London St. Pancras through Cromford station on 15th June 1911. The Midland's 'Peak' line between Manchester and Derby was notable for serving the estates of several members of the aristocracy, landed gentry and industrialists and stations of suitable grandeur were provided for them. At Cromford it was the Arkwright family of Willersley Castle, who had made their money in the cotton industry, for whom provision was made. The station buildings have an Alpine flavour appropriate in a part of the country known as 'Little Switzerland'.

Derby 9561

An outstanding London & North Western Railway official photograph taken at Rugby, at 4.01pm on 30th July 1896. A northbound express, headed by three cylinder compound 2-(2-2)-0 No.1370 locomotive *City of Glasgow*, probably the 2.10pm from London Euston to Mancester and Liverpool, waits at a busy platform of this important station. The driver and his fireman relax, whilst a substantial amount of luggage, including a bicycle, is loaded and unloaded. The 15 × 12ins glass plate has registered the fine detail of the station 'furniture', including a splendid array of signs, some impressive gas lamps, a weighing machine, a bookstall and a couple of 'next train' departure clocks.

Crewe A 314

The chimneys of Halifax rise above a busy station on 30th August
1912. On the right a Lancashire & Yorkshire Railway westbound
local train awaits departure; alongside it an express is ready to leave.
A rake of Lancashire & Yorkshire coaches is at the central platform,
with a North Eastern Railway train opposite and in the foreground a
permanent way gang has halted its labours for the company
photographer. The line was built on a rising gradient eastwards
through the town and the catch points signposted at the end of the
platform were intended to derail runaway vehicles before they
'escaped'. Halifax was an important centre in the wool industry but
outside the station on the right was Mackintosh's confectionery
factory whose chimney dominates the immediate scene.

Horwich F 1026

York station is the subject of this superb study taken by H. Gordon Tidey in the early 1920s, from Locomotive Yard Signal Box. A Lancashire & Yorkshire Railway 4-4-2 locomotive is departing with an express to Manchester and Liverpool while a North Eastern Railway 4-4-0 stands on the through line beneath the forest of semaphore signals at the south end of the station. Off the picture to the left are the South sheds and on the right can be seen the Queen Street shed used by the LYR, one of whose 4-6-0s is standing outside the building. To the immediate right of the station are carriage sidings leading through an arch cut through the city's mediaeval walls to the original York station. York Minster stands guard over the scene and remains to this day the tallest building in the city.

Tidey 9341

An Inter-City High Speed Train heading north from York station in January 1985, pictured by a National Railway Museum photographer recording the aftermath of a snowstorm. The 125mph HST, introduced in 1976, revolutionised British Railways' express services throughout Britain.

NRM 60/85

Cyril Herbert's 1938 study, 'Lines of communication', taken at King's Cross station, was submitted to members of the Leica Postal Portfolio photographic society for comment and criticism. It generally received a favourable response, although one member said that there were "too many lines" and another "This is one of those prints which strike me as very clever, but not beautiful".

Herbert R05 A5/7

'Southern Electric' reads the hoarding, with its distinctive 'flash', by the side of Liss station in 1939 and sums up that company's forward-looking policy of adopting modern traction on its most intensely-worked routes. The Portsmouth line electrification was completed in 1937. The train consists of a pair of '2-BIL' electric multiple units which entered service in 1935. Box was one of the few amateur photographers of the 1930s who produced images of the new electric trains.

Box 403

Bury Bolton Street station in Lancashire & Yorkshire Railway days.
This official photograph was taken on 26th May 1915 during the first
year of the 'Great War' and mixed with tourist advertisements are
stirring recruiting posters displayed under the canopy, including
'Remember Scarborough' and 'Enlist Now'. The former referred to the
incident the previous December when the resort had been shelled by
German ships, the first attack on British shores for over 100 years.
Bury was the home of the Lancashire Fusiliers who were to win
eighteen Victoria Crosses during the war, more than any other
regiment, including the famous "six VCs before breakfast" at
Gallipoli. The station burned down in 1947 and was replaced by a
building of typical 1950s modern style which today forms the
headquarters of the preserved East Lancashire Railway.

Horwich F 1808

Light and shade at Waterloo
on 21st May 1938 as the
4.30pm to Bournemouth
awaits departure behind a
Southern Railway 'Schools'
class 4-4-0 locomotive. The
glass roof and end screens
bear the tell-tale signs of
steam-age soot, contrasting
with the third rail of the
clean new electric era.

Box 196

The 'parachute' water tank at Bray station, on the Dublin & South Eastern line, affords an unusual but opportune advertising site — though presumably 0-6-2T locomotive No.673 is not being filled with soda water! The positioning of the signal is of interest, almost on the road, where it can be clearly seen by the train crew without being obscured by the water tank and station buildings.

Click A1/139

Many railway stations contain outstanding architectural features, from castellated fronts and classical colonnades to glass roofs and clock towers. Norwich Thorpe station boasts this fine dome above the passenger concourse, photographed for the Great Eastern Railway in 1913.

Stratford 1032

Two diesel multiple unit trains pass each other at Betws-y-Coed station on the single line Conway Valley branch between Llandudno Junction and Blaenau Ffestiniog on 28th July 1960. A Pullman camping coach stands in the sidings beyond the far platform. The conversion to diesel operation proved popular with passengers, for the new units were a considerable improvement on the ageing compartment carriages they replaced. Enthusiasts, however, preferred steam and images of modern traction like this one were more often than not the work of official photographers.

Euston DM 7038

The London & North Western and the Great Western Railways both
built branches to Blaenau Ffestiniog to exploit the lucrative slate
traffic and this LNWR photograph was taken at the height of the
town's prosperity during the building boom of the 1880s. It shows, in
spectacular fashion, how railways and the industries they served
could devastate the landscape, with the shattered mountain and the
Diphwys Casson quarry tips dominating the town below. The
Rhiwbach No.2 incline, eventually the last operational gravity incline
in North Wales, can be seen on the mountainside. A GWR train can
be seen at the company's station while in the foreground is the
Newborough Slate Mill, which supplied school writing tablets and
was served by a branch of the narrow gauge Festiniog Railway.

Crewe MC 66

One of the few narrow gauge railways built primarily for passenger use was the Lynton & Barnstaple Railway in Devon, which served an area on the remote fringes of Exmoor. The 1ft 11½ins gauge line climbed to 700 ft above sea level to its terminus at Lynton. It opened in 1898, but lost money for nearly all its life and closed in 1935. This photograph by Godfrey Soole was taken early in the line's final summer and shows the 2-6-2T locomotive No.188, *Lew*, leaving with the 6.07pm to Barnstaple. Although the railway remained popular with holidaymakers in the summer months, few local people patronised it by this time.

Soole 831

One of Britain's classic railway structures is the Royal Border Bridge at Berwick-upon-Tweed. With 28 arches and a maximum height above the Tweed of 126ft, the bridge was formally opened by Queen Victoria and Prince Albert in 1850 and provided the last link in the East Coast route between London and Scotland. Crossing the bridge towards Berwick station on 12th August 1949 is LNER A3 4-6-2 locomotive No.60043 *Brown Jack* with a northbound stopping train. Not surprisingly, the setting of the Royal Border Bridge has inspired both photographers and poster artists over the years.

LPC 23997 (Wethersett)

Sunrise on the former Great Central line. John Click has caught the early morning mist rising from the fields as a Class K3 2-6-0 locomotive heads north with a train of cattle vans.

Click 1/63

The 22-arch viaduct at Stockport, on the Manchester & Birmingham Railway, was completed in 1842 and carried two tracks across the River Mersey. The growth of traffic under the London & North Western Railway in the 1870s and 1880s led the company to widen the viaduct to take two more tracks. Here the widening of the piers is in progress — note how the mill on the right is being partially demolished to allow for the extra width of the structure. The viaduct still stands and the railway is as busy as ever, but the mills have mostly gone and the M63 motorway traffic roars beneath.

Crewe MC 110

A Devon branch which saw heavy summer traffic was that from Newton Abbot to Paignton and Kingswear where a ferry provided a connection with Dartmouth. Through holiday services from London and the north brought the largest express locomotives to the branch, but this is a local service crossing Churston Viaduct behind a '41xx' class 2-6-2T locomotive during the summer of 1959.

Earley 23/59

The Forth Bridge is undoubtedly Britain's most famous railway landmark and its distinctive cantilever design is recognisable instantly throughout the world. Opened in 1890, it completed the East Coast railway route between London and Aberdeen. Frank Box's photograph (opposite) of 21st September 1938 shows how a freight train is dwarfed by the massive cantilevers at the Inchgarvie pier in the middle of the Forth. R. D. Stephen took a series of detailed photographs of the bridge in the 1930s, some from seemingly precarious positions. These show the heart-stopping view from up in the girders looking towards South Queensferry.

Stephen FB 17

Stephen FB 29

Box 343

Northbound trains out of London's King's Cross station faced a
difficult start to their journeys on a rising gradient and through
tunnels. A London & North Eastern Railway express is about to enter
Copenhagen Tunnel behind Class A3 4-6-2 locomotive No.51 *Blink
Bonny* on 7th June 1947. The leading vehicle is in the LNER's
distinctive varnished teak finish, with a passenger reading his
newspaper in the corridor. The scene around Copenhagen Tunnel
will be familiar to fans of the Ealing Studios classic comedy *The
Ladykillers* for it was here where the villains pursued each other in
the final sequences.

LPC 25345 (Wethersett)

The A4 class 4-6-2 locomotive No.60017 *Silver Fox* leaves Welwyn's South Tunnel with the 'Tees-Tyne Pullman' service from London King's Cross to Darlington and Newcastle in the summer of 1955. The journey north took 4 hours 11 minutes, which was considered fast for a steam-hauled train, and the service proved popular with north-eastern businessmen visiting the capital.

Earley 85/55

EM1 class electric locomotive No 26047, designed for use on the steep gradients of the Manchester to Sheffield line, leaves the new Woodhead Tunnel through the Pennines with a freight train in 1956.

Ransome-Wallis 11879

A Class B16 4-6-0 locomotive with a down freight train crosses the swing bridge over the River Ouse at Naburn, near York, in August 1957, in an image taken by J. F. Henton, a member of the Railway Photographic Society.

Henton B16

An ex-North Eastern Railway Class J72 0-6-0T locomotive No.68735 trundles over Scarborough Bridge across the Ouse at York working a local freight round to the terminal at Foss Islands. A shunter is riding on the running board of the locomotive — in contravention of the rules!

The bridge is not the original cast iron structure from the opening of the York-Scarborough line in 1845 but a wrought iron replacement completed in 1875. Landmarks still familiar today are Lendal road bridge, the Guildhall and the tower of St. Martin-le-Grand church. The date of the photograph is 15th August 1948.

LPC 24560 (Wethersett)

Few railway bridges occupy a more scenic location than the
Barmouth Bridge, on the Cambrian Coast line to Pwllheli. The bridge
extends some 800 yards across the Mawddach estuary on 113 timber
piers with eight iron spans at the Barmouth end including a rolling
section which was designed to be drawn back to clear a channel for
shipping. A small bridge on the near shore allows the Barmouth
lifeboat slipway to pass under the railway. This photograph by Dr. T.
F. Budden was taken before the rebuilding of the iron section in
1899.

LGRP 21247

In the 1870s the London & North Western Railway began work on quadrupling the track on the approach to Liverpool's Lime Street station. The task was a daunting one and involved excavating down to the top of the original tunnel, which had been built in the 1820s. Stone recovered from the new cutting built to accommodate the additional track was used for construction of the bridges and retaining walls. A series of remarkable photographs in the Crewe collection recalls the scale of the undertaking. The photograph above shows a bridge being constructed on the cut-and-cover method over the new lines in about 1881, while the image opposite gives an idea of the depth of the excavation and shows a locomotive hauling wagons carrying away the spoil. The project was completed and the new tracks opened to traffic in 1885 — and most of the work had been done by hand!

Crewe MC 25

Part Four

HANDLING
THE TRAFFIC

The railways were adept at
meeting the demands of
special events, often on a
large scale. When the Royal
Agricultural Society show
was staged at Derby in June
1906 the Midland Railway
added to its existing sidings
at Osmaston Park and
provided a complete goods
depot to serve the event.
This view shows the goods
dock, capable of handling
two twenty-wagon trains
simultaneously. The MR
dealt with around 1,300
wagons of exhibits for the
show and more than 700
wagons conveying livestock.

Derby 1445

Waterloo is London's busiest station and is pictured here at its most crowded, as holidaymakers queue for trains on the Southern Railway's services to the West Country in the summer of 1946. The photograph was taken to show how holiday traffic had returned to normal with the end of the Second World War.

NRM 547/83

Manchester Victoria was the principal station on the Lancashire &
Yorkshire Railway system. This animated scene shows Saturday
crowds boarding a train for Blackpool and only a few have stayed
still long enough to register on the negative. By 27th August 1927
when this photograph was taken the LYR lines had become part of
the London, Midland & Scottish Railway and the tank locomotive
passing through the station on the left carries LMS livery. Note the
sign urging passengers to have their 'Tickets and Contracts Ready';
'Contracts' was how the LYR and some other companies referred to
what are now known as season tickets.

Horwich F 4145

A 'passenger' posed in the window of a carriage of a London, Midland & Scottish train at Euston station in 1931. This official photograph was taken to advertise the LMS's reservation facilities.

LMS 6013

A surreal still life of items held at Paddington station's Lost Property Office on 19th October 1933.

GWR B 10641

Savernake station, Great Western Railway, is an excellent example of the country junction where the branch line joins the main line. 'Star' class 4-6-0 locomotive No.4035 *Queen Charlotte*, with a London-bound express, is running into the station where the Marlborough branch train is waiting in the bay platform to make a connection. A couple of porters are ready to load mailbags into the London train, while a group of schoolgirls appears to have been the branch train's major payload. Frank Box took this photograph at about 4.30pm on 29th July 1938.

Box 253

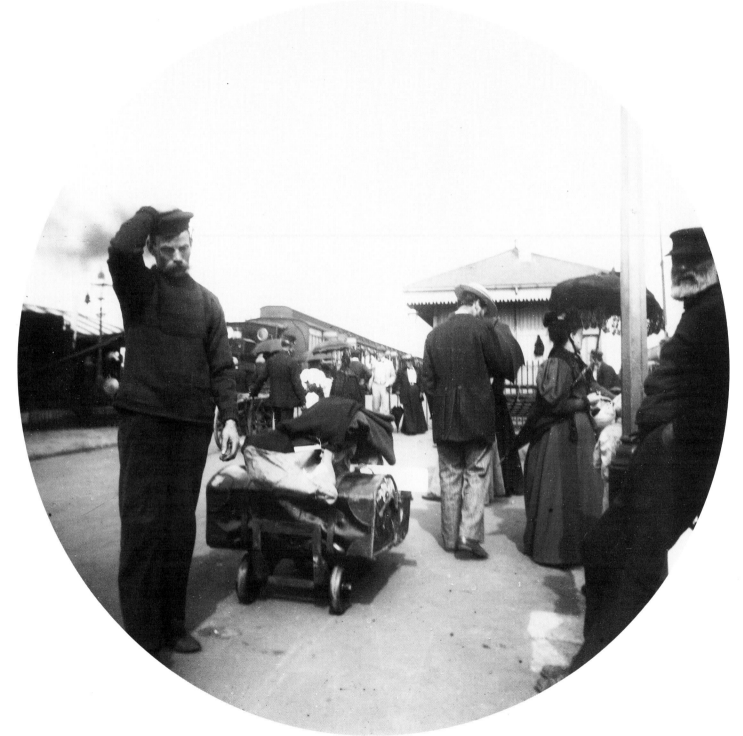

A Great Western Railway 'boat train' meets the Channel Islands ferry at Weymouth quay in about 1900. The connecting service which, unusually, ran through the town's streets, made it possible to complete the journey from London to Guernsey in twelve hours. This image, by an unknown photographer, was taken with a Kodak No.2 box camera which produced characteristic circular negatives on a sixty exposure roll film. The inventor of the Kodak No.2, George Eastman, had promised, "You press the button, we do the rest" and with the introduction of the camera amateur photographers no longer needed their own darkrooms. When the film had been completed the camera was returned to the manufacturers, who processed the negatives and provided prints.

Anderson 13

In the 1890s it was unusual for official photographers to record
celebrities who travelled by rail, but on 28th July 1894 the Midland
Railway photographer pictured the famous French actress Sarah
Bernhardt — in the centre — and her entourage at London St.
Pancras station. They are standing in front of a special saloon
carriage which could be hired by private parties. Sarah Bernhardt
was born in 1845 and, despite a convent education, pursued a
colourful career on the stage in Europe, America, Australia and even
Russia. She frequently appeared in London and was on friendly terms
with the Prince of Wales, later Edward VII.

Derby 610

Passengers disembarking onto a tender from the White Star liner SS *Cedric*, at the London & North Western Railway's Holyhead harbour in 1909.

LMS 1880

In 1921 the Lancashire & Yorkshire Railway official photographer took a series of fascinating views of Manchester street scenes. Quite why these photographs were taken is not known, but it is possible that some of them were used as illustrations in the carriage panels which adorned compartments. This is Oxford Street looking towards Oxford Road station. A Manchester Corporation tram is proceeding towards Sale, a destination also served by the MSJA railway line. The railway paid rates to the corporation and were annoyed that some of this revenue subsidised the trams, which were eroding their local passenger traffic.

Horwich F 3118

In the first months of the Second World War it was feared that major cities would become the immediate targets of aerial bombardment and the four main railway companies played a significant role in the evacuation of children to areas considered safe. There was a second wave of evacuations when France fell in June 1940 when the Great Western Railway ran 96 special trains, conveying nearly 70,000 children from London to the countryside. Labelled and carrying a few belongings and their gas masks, children escorted by their teachers and a nurse arrive at the GWR's Maidenhead station in Berkshire.

Paddington E363

Waterloo in wartime, 1943. The roof has been blacked out and the lamps shaded as hurrying figures, many clearly on military business, are silhouetted against rare shafts of light. In the foreground two policemen talk to a soldier. Waterloo did not escape unscathed during the war, but mostly managed to maintain what passed for "business as usual". To counter the contemporary gloom, programmes of music were broadcast over the loudspeakers.

NRM 1155/6/63

A pair of North Eastern Railway Stirling petrol-engined motor buses present an incongruous spectacle as they disturb the tranquillity of the village street at Beeford in the East Riding of Yorkshire. There was a large area of agricultural country, bounded by Bridlington, Driffield, Beverley and Hornsea, untapped by rail communication. The NER served the area with motor buses, three of which it brought from Stirling Motor Carriages Ltd. A service between Beverley and Beeford began in September 1903, one of the first operated by a railway company. The NER buses took 1 hour 50 minutes for the fourteen-mile journey on the poor roads of the time.

Horwich F 207

A Lancashire & Yorkshire
Railway cart delivering
finished cloth to a
wholesaler in Southmill
Street, Manchester, on New
Year's Eve 1912 while its
horse takes refreshment. The
Lancashire cotton industry
consumed over two million
tons of raw cotton a year, the
LYR often handling it four
times between its arrival in
Liverpool and its completion
as cloth for sale. In the right
background is Manchester
Town Hall, an outstanding
example of Victorian
extravagance emphasising
the city's industrial wealth
and importance.

Horwich F 1131

Country lorry services were developed during the 1920s for the delivery of goods from a railhead to its outlying areas. Newbury was one of the districts in which lorry services were introduced by the Great Western Railway in 1929. On 24th September that year this Associated Daimler vehicle was delivering agricultural produce to this picturesque thatched cottage deep in rural Berkshire.

GWR B Box 211/5

Midland Railway battery-powered delivery vans having their accumulators charged at St. Pancras goods depot on 11th July 1917.

Derby 10641

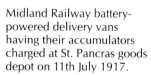

A busy quayside at the London & North Western Railway's docks at Garston, Liverpool, in 1913. Dockers are unloading bananas from the SS *Aracataca*, sorting them by size and packing them in straw for transport to the fruit and vegetable markets.

LMS 3028

The coming of the railways made it possible for national newspapers to reach breakfast tables throughout the land just a few hours after they had been printed. The Great Western Railway set its photographers a challenge in recording the traffic, for this photograph was taken at Paddington station just after midnight on 10th December 1910. The output of Fleet Street is illuminated by the flash of the GWR's cameraman as it is loaded on vans to be raced to the West Country.

GWR B 557

At the beginning of the Second World War Malvern College was one of a number of buildings identified by the authorities as suitable for the evacuation of Government offices. To provide for this contingency the school itself was therefore evacuated to the opulent surroundings of Blenheim Palace. In the event nothing happened — apart from the occupation of two of the school houses by Wrens and some Free French cadets — and on 28th July 1940 Malvern College began to return home. 140 tons of school property, including furniture and gymnasium equipment, were removed and GWR staff, assisted by some of the older boys from the school, are seen here loading covered lorries.

GWR B 13996

Railway wagons deliver coal and raw materials to Millom Ironworks in Cumberland in November 1952. The photograph was taken for *Men of the Rocks*, a filmstrip made by British Transport Films. The filmstrip touched only briefly on transport, for it was primarily about geology and the landscape. Drawing attention to Black Combe Fell looming over the works, the lecture notes asked "Could any picture show more clearly how the iron towns depend on the rock; or how close they are to some of the wildest scenery in England?".

BTF 1981

Cider apples are unloaded from wagons at Bulmer's factory in Hereford, in a scene from the British Transport Films' production *Railway Freight*, made in 1957.

BTF 3447

Midland Railway porters unload milk for Londoners' tables at the Somers Town fish and milk dock alongside St. Pancras station. The churns had a capacity of 17 gallons and required two men to manoeuvre them from the special ventilated wagons. The railways precipitated a major shift in the urban diet and by the 1890s when this photograph was taken they were supplying about 50 million gallons of milk a year to London alone.

Derby 030

The Severn Tunnel, at 4 miles 628 yards, is the longest in Britain and when opened in 1886 by the Great Western Railway provided a direct line to South Wales instead of the previous roundabout route via Gloucester. The line descends steadily from both directions into the tunnel where it reaches the lowest point on a British railway, 144ft below sea level. In this photograph, taken by Godfrey Soole in the 1930s, a GWR '31xx' 2-6-2T locomotive No.3169 is assisting a '28xx' 2-8-0 goods engine up the 1 in 100 gradient from the eastern end of the tunnel towards Pilning with a heavy freight train.

Soole 500

Somers Town goods depot, next to St. Pancras station in London's Euston Road, was the Midland Railway's main London freight terminal. This official photograph, dating from about 1894, shows the loading dock where goods were transferred between road and rail. On the right are railway wagons and vans, shunted into bays where portable signposts identify their departure points or destinations. On the left are the road vehicles used to deliver goods to and from the depot. The site is now occupied by the British Library.

Derby 3026

The 'merry-go-round' train is a method of transporting coal to power stations developed in the late 1960s. A train of hopper wagons runs direct from the coalfield, passing slowly but without stopping through the power station with the coal being emptied through automatically-operated bottom discharge doors. This is Didcot power station in July 1973, its cooling towers dominating Class 45 locomotive No.163 and its train.

Williams   10295

Wensleydale, in North Yorkshire, is a major centre for dairy production and the opening of a branch line from Northallerton enabled milk to be quickly transported from the farm to consumers in towns and cities. The Wensleydale Pure Milk Society was formed as a co-operative of dairy farmers and in 1905 took the rental of a bottling plant built by the North Eastern Railway at Northallerton. On 26th April 1927 dairymen are seen pushing the 'Cream Special', a four-wheel trolley carrying milk churns and cream cans from the dairy for return to the Dales stations. A red flag on a pole denotes its presence instead of the more usual front and tail lamps.

Household 327

A perennial problem at Manchester Victoria station was the volume of parcels traffic and luggage to be handled. The Lancashire & Yorkshire Railway's Chief Mechanical Engineer John Aspinall tackled it in an ingenious way when he devised an overhead conveyor suspended from the roof which ran from the parcels office on the north side across the full width of the station. Erected in 1898, the carrier was soon running some ten miles and moving 1,000 basketloads a week. The job of driver was not for the faint-hearted but after an accident in which a worker on a carriage roof was knocked off by the basket and killed when the carrier was travelling backwards, a more substantial perch was provided so that the operator faced forward at all times. The overhead conveyor was damaged when the station was hit during the 'Manchester Blitz' in December 1940 and was subsequently removed.

Horwich F878

A number of landed gentlemen laid 15ins gauge railways on their
estates, ostensibly for the transport of materials but doubtless also for
pleasure! After the First World War Sir Robert Walker re-opened the
railway on his estate at Sand Hutton near York, converting the 15in
gauge line he had commenced in 1912 to 18ins. The Sand Hutton
Railway ran for $7\frac{1}{4}$ miles to connect with the North Eastern Railway at
Warthill. The rolling stock came from the Deptford Meat Railway and
was used for transporting goods and farm produce. A branch was
also provided to serve the Claxton Brickworks, where this
photograph was taken on 19th February 1928, when coal was being
delivered for the kilns. After Sir Robert Walker's death in 1930 the
Sand Hutton Railway went into decline and closed in 1932.

Household 616

A sea of coal at Aintree yard, near Liverpool, on 26th April 1911
vividly demonstrates how important freight traffic was to the
railways. The Lancashire & Yorkshire Railway transported two million
tons of coal a year to Liverpool both for export and the bunkering of
steamships. Aintree was one of two storage yards provided by the
LYR on the outskirts of the port and held 3,000 wagons. Most of the
coal wagons were owned by collieries or coal merchants.

Horwich F 868

Part Five

THE DAILY
ROUND

A platelaying gang takes a
brief rest for the camera
whilst replacing track at
Wickwar in Gloucestershire
on the Midland Railway's
main line to Bristol, during
the 1890s. Their work is
supervised by the company's
engineers and attracts the
gaze of a party of villagers
halted in the lane alongside
the track.

Derby 4076

'Engineman', Cyril Herbert's portrait of the driver of the 'Battle of Britain' class locomotive *Sir Frederick Pile*. Taken in April 1948 it was submitted to the Leica Postal Portfolios circle. It was well received, although some members of the group commented that too much prominence was given to the locomotive number and that the driver's cap cast an unsightly shadow over his eyes.

Herbert R28 B4 26

The driver and fireman on the footplate of the 4-6-0 'Schools' class locomotive No.30913 *Christ's Hospital* at Ramsgate, lit by the glow of the firebox in this night photograph by Dr. Patrick Ransome-Wallis. The fireman shovels coal, while the driver has his hand on the regulator, which acts as a throttle by controlling the flow of steam to the cylinders.

Ransome-Wallis 9532

At the beginning of the Second World War there was considerable fear of poison gas attacks so respirators, or 'gas masks' as they were popularly known, were issued to every civilian. Railwaymen were given heavy duty versions, as their work put them at greater risk during air attacks. Here a driver demonstrates the wearing of a respirator on the footplate of a Great Western Railway 'Castle' class locomotive. Steel helmets were also standard issue.

GWR B348/15

The driver and fireman of a London, Brighton & South Coast Railway
4-4-2 locomotive, dating from 1905. The low tender provided a good
vantage point for the photographer, but left the crew exposed to the
elements. A storm sheet could be lashed across from the cab roof to
the tender in adverse weather but the protection afforded was
minimal.

The cabs of different types of locomotive varied only in detail and
the basic controls were largely the same. The regulator handle
dominates the centre of the firebox backplate, while behind the
driver's shoulder on the left is the brake handle. In the centre are the
two injector handles for filling the boiler with water and the two
gauges which show the water level in the boiler. The boiler pressure
and other gauges are mounted on the cab sides. Above the firehole
door is the shelf mainly intended to keep the oil cans warm; of
course, it also proved ideal for keeping cans of tea hot!

Burtt 1201

A London, Midland & Scottish Railway 4-6-0 locomotive at Longsight depot, Manchester, in 1936. A locomotive in traffic had its fire dropped at regular intervals — every seven or eight days, perhaps, for express passenger classes — for a boiler wash-out and examination. Once the locomotive had cooled sufficiently the boilersmith entered the firebox to check the condition of the stays, tubeplate and firebars. Fittings in the smokebox were also examined and repairs to boiler fittings were carried out when the locomotive was out of steam.

LMS 8008

Four members of the crew of an engineers' train enjoying a break in the magnificent scenery near Glenfinnan, on the West Highland extension line between Fort William and Mallaig, on 13th August 1950. The locomotive is a Class K2 2-6-0 No.61786, built by the London & North Eastern Railway for use on the West Highland lines where its power was used to good effect on the difficult gradients. The steam crane is being used to unload concrete drainage pipes. The reason for the bicycle is not immediately obvious, but the photographer, the Reverend Arthur Cawston, was taking a cycling holiday.

Cawston LNER 329

A posed publicity shot of a W. H. Smith 'station boy' selling newspapers and magazines to passengers on a London & North Western Railway train at Euston in about 1904. In 1848 Smith's obtained an exclusive contract to operate bookstalls on LNWR stations and by 1890 employed over 3,500 'station boys' to sell on the platforms. Following a dispute over increased rents their contract was terminated at the end of 1905.

LMS 369

This photograph is one of a sequence taken to illustrate the refreshment services which the Great Western Railway provided for its passengers at London's Paddington station in 1915. In all the others the carriages in the background are static, but when this image was taken the train began to move off and, blurred by the long exposure required, effectively conveys a sense of motion. It is not clear whether this was the photographer's intention, or merely a happy accident.

GWR B998

Tommy, seen here with his 'driver', A. C. Newton, at Newmarket in 1963, was one of the last shunting horses employed by British Railways. He is hauling a horse box, used to transport racehorses from the Newmarket stables to meetings across the country. Shunting horses were withdrawn from British Railways shortly after this photograph was taken.

Clapham 1545/63

In a graphic, if somewhat bizarre, attempt to illustrate the level of injuries to the Great Eastern Railway's horses on London streets, nails recovered from their feet were annually hung in strips of leather. A railwayman at the Bishopsgate Horse Infirmary in 1911 demonstrates this unconventional indicator of the company's economic activities.

Stratford 1114

Rats and mice were a perennial problem in warehouses, stores, stations and signal boxes so ratcatchers were numbered amongst the railway staff. Here Jim Forty and Alfred Greenwin show off the traps and poisons of their trade in St. Pancras goods yard in 1953, along with their canine assistants Jill, Sally and Tiny and a selection of rats who did not get away.

Euston D 1336

The maintenance of the permanent way is essential to the safe
running of the railway. Here a ganger is patrolling his 'length' on the
main line near Manningtree, Essex, in May 1948. He is checking the
condition of sleepers, the fastenings of the chairs holding the rails,
the tightness of fishplates joining the rails together and the size of the
expansion gap between rails. He carries a long-handled hammer for
knocking in loose keys securing the rails in their chairs.

The photographer, Cyril Herbert, was one of the few enthusiasts
who produced studies of railwaymen. Herbert worked on the
railways himself and this one was taken while on duty.

Herbert M 4813-3

A lampman changing the oil lamps which illuminate the spectacle lenses of semaphore signals at Lancaster in 1936. The lamps burned for eight days and were changed once a week, the lampman following a 'beat' which brought him to each signal on his round on a regular basis. Fresh lamps were taken up to the signal and the old ones brought down for filling and trimming. 'Lamping' was not a job for the faint-hearted; signal posts could be quite tall and could sway about a bit!

LMS 7507

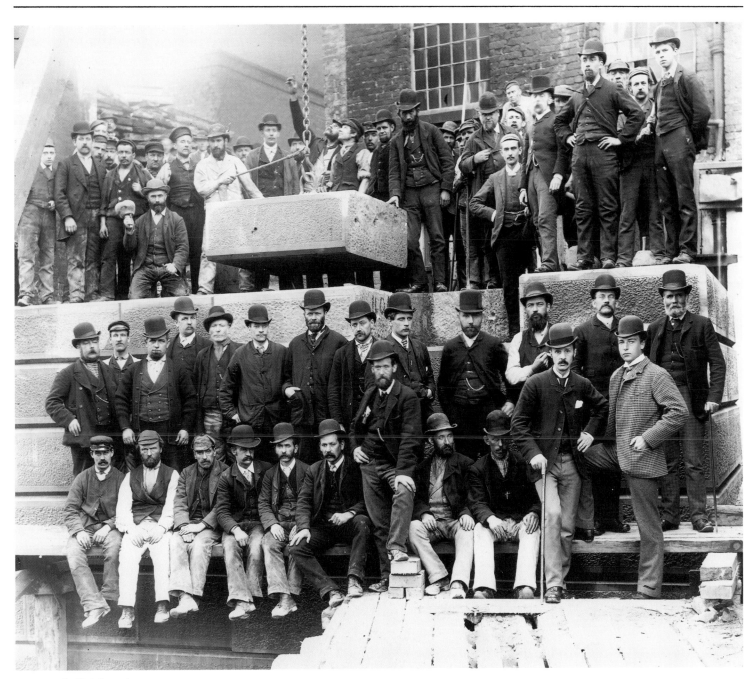

A group of officials and
workmen pose for the
London & North Western
Railway photographer as a
stone is lowered during
construction of the base of
one of the piers when the
Stockport Viaduct was
widened in the 1880s.

Crewe MC 115

During both world wars
women were taken on by the
railways to release men for
service in the forces.
Although the jobs of many
railwaymen were classed as
'reserved occupations',
women were employed on a
wide range of duties. Here
women on the Great
Western Railway are oiling
points in the goods sidings at
Reading on 12th March
1943 under the watchful eye
of a look-out, whose
function was to watch for
approaching trains and warn
the track workers to stand
clear. By the outbreak of war
some 26,000 women were
employed by the railways
but by 1944 the number had
risen to 114,000.

GWR B14259

Cyril Herbert carried his
camera at all times when he
was working on the line and
took as much interest in the
forms and shapes which
resulted from railway
construction as in the
glamorous express
locomotives which passed
him. This scene shows a
London & North Eastern
Railway civil engineering
gang at work at Holloway on
15th May 1933.

Herbert R1 102/17

In the early years of the twentieth century railway companies delivered direct to the home, office or factory and they operated large fleets of road vehicles. These came in all shapes and sizes and included this chain-driven Oldsmobile used by the London & North Western Railway's motor cartage inspectors in 1907.

LMS 820

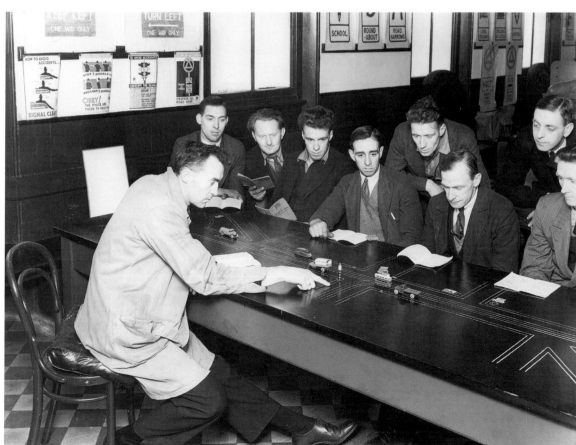

Road delivery was an important feature of the railways' freight services and here are some London, Midland & Scottish Railway van drivers attending a course on road safety at Sutton Park, near Birmingham, in 1937. Note the walls adorned with road signs and the use of childrens' toys as instructional models.

LMS   8275

Platemaking in the accumulator shop at Wolverton on 10th March 1930. Accumulators were used to supply electric lighting in carriages.

Wolverton   W73

An errant worker literally 'on the carpet' in the office at the Great Western Railway's Paddington goods depot in 1928. The reason this staged photograph was taken is not clear, but it was part of a major sequence covering operations at the depot and was perhaps intended to discourage theft or minor misdemeanours. The walls of the manager's office are decorated with GWR official photographs and posters.

GWR   B-Box 201/9

The larger railway works included laboratories where staff undertook scientific research and evaluated damaged components and new products. This official photograph was taken at the Swindon Works laboratory on 14th September 1927.

GWR F3/56

The booking office at Watford Junction on the London, Midland & Scottish Railway in September 1943. Stocks of tickets of the most requested destinations are held in racks ready to be date-stamped in a press on issue to a passenger. For well over one hundred years railways relied on the pre-printed cardboard ticket. Blank tickets were kept for more unusual destinations and the booking clerk completed these by hand. A large range of printed tickets had to be kept in stock, including first and third class, single and return, adult and child, as well as a whole range of special and concessionary tickets such as those for workmen, servicemen and dogs.

LMS 9281

The drawing office of Stratford Works, Great Eastern Railway c1910. Drawings are being prepared with the aid of rulers, compasses and set squares. The draughtsmen have the benefit of electric lights which can be lowered and raised on pulleys.

Stratford 700

The kitchen of the restaurant car of the 'Norfolk Coast Express', which ran between Liverpool Street and Cromer on the Great Eastern Railway. This 1910 view shows how the railways made the best use of limited space to prepare food on the train. Wooden racks secure the plates while cups and milk jugs hang from hooks in the ceiling. On the table at the left is a bottle of the GER's own blend of 'East Anglian' whisky. Luncheons prepared in this kitchen cost 2s 6d (12½p) and up to 36 first and 72 third class passengers were served at any one time.

Stratford 793

Many tasks were performed in railway workshops which one might not immediately associate with the construction and repair of locomotives and rolling stock. The Great Eastern Railway's works at Stratford contained a sewing machine shop and these women are working on carriage blinds. On the end of the bench on the left are some leather straps for lowering carriage windows. Although women ventured into the engineering shops out of necessity during the First World War, by the time of this 1921 view 'normal' duties had been restored.

Stratford 372

During the First World War Soldiers' and Sailors' Free Buffets were established at major stations where large numbers of servicemen passed through. The cost was met by donations and they were staffed twenty-four hours a day by women volunteers. This official Great Western Railway photograph shows the Free Buffet at Paddington station in London, with the portraits of King George V and the British lion surveying the scene.

GWR B 2035

The Great Western Railway had recruited over 16,000 women by 1943 and they proved to be a highly-adaptable workforce, to the surprise of many foremen who at first showed some prejudice against their employment. Here a female mechanic is servicing a Thornycroft delivery van at the Alfred Road Garage, Paddington, on 28th May 1942.

GWR B Box 377/29

Much of the work involved in the operation and maintenance of steam locomotives was unglamorous, dirty and unpleasant. Some of the worst tasks were the emptying of ash from the firebox and smokebox, shown in this shot by Maurice Earley taken at Camden depot in 1955. A fireman is clearing the smokebox of his LMS 'Jubilee' class 4-6-0 locomotive, shovelling the ash into tubs running on a narrow gauge railway. The tubs were hoisted into an overhead hopper which held the ash until it was unloaded into wagons for dispersal. The fine particles of unburned coal were prone to blow about, so a hosepipe spray is being used to keep down the dust. The poor working conditions with minimal lighting, fire-irons strewn hazardously on the ground and grime everywhere were, by the 1950s, an important factor in the railways' increasing difficulties in recruiting and retaining staff.

Earley 97/55

4-6-0 locomotive *Kenilworth Castle*, framed in an arch at Old Oak Common locomotive depot by Maurice Earley in 1956.

Earley F30/8

'Jubilee' class 4-6-0 locomotive No.45697 *Achilles* in Holbeck shed in Leeds during the early 1960s. The locomotives ranged around the turntable and shafts of light cutting through the gloom, smoke and steam made the shed scene particularly photogenic. It was a subject to which the photographer Eric Treacy returned again and again.

Treacy 35/1/181

Flats overlook locomotives ranged around the turntable at Ranelagh Bridge depot, near London's Paddington station, in 1953. 4-6-0 locomotive No.6016 *King Edward V* moves onto the turntable, while Nos.5993 *Kirby Hall* and 6976 *Graythwaite Hall* wait their turn with other engines. The photographer at bottom right has a twin lens reflex rollfilm camera mounted on a tripod.

Earley 26/53

Fiery conditions as the furnace is tapped in the steel foundry at the
Lancashire & Yorkshire Railway's Horwich Works in August 1919.
The railway companies preferred to be self-sufficient and their works
encompassed the complete range of manufacturing processes. Even
relatively small companies, like the LYR, had their own foundries.

Horwich F 2776

A boilermaker uses a pneumatic riveter in the assembly of a firebox
at the London & North Eastern Railway's Stratford Works, on 12th
November 1936. While not originally intended as an 'art' portrait, it
clearly shows the skill of the official photographer and resembles the
work of other, more celebrated, practitioners of social realism, such
as the American photographer Lewis Hine.

Stratford 1773

Boilermakers assembling fireboxes for '1093' and '11' class locomotives at the Lancashire & Yorkshire Railway's Horwich Works in about 1905. The rivets are being heated in the furnace on the left and then positioned by 'holders-up' for their colleagues to strike them home with hammers.

Horwich F 223

Coppersmiths making steam dome and safety valve covers at the Great Western Railway's Swindon Works on 8th August 1938.

GWR F3/145

A row of newly-turned Great
Eastern Railway carriage
wheels at the company's
works in about 1912. The
wheels were machined on
the lathes, powered by the
belts running from overhead
drive shafts, seen on the left.

Stratford 927

Class 40 and 47 diesel-
electric locomotives are
overhauled at Crewe Works
in the 1960s. Although the
locomotives have changed,
in many ways this scene
differs little from official
photographs of the works
taken in the early years of
the twentieth century.

Gorton 66370

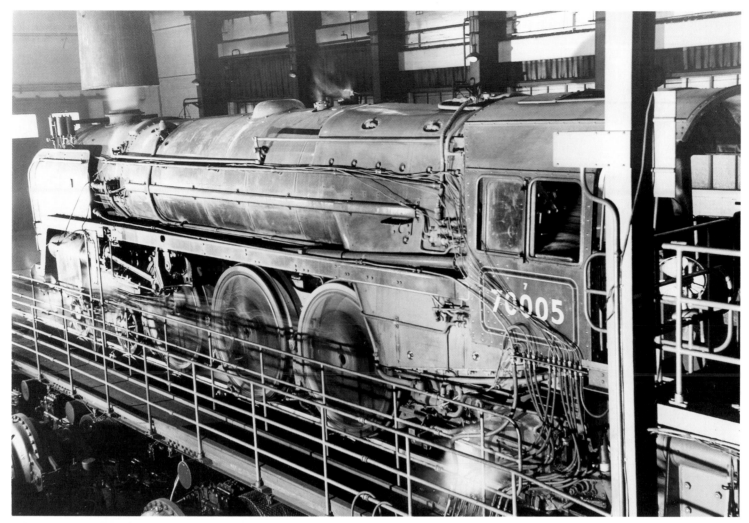

A locomotive working flat out, but going nowhere: the 'Britannia' class 4-6-2 locomotive *John Milton* on the test rig at British Railways' Rugby Locomotive Testing Station in the early 1950s. The engine runs on rollers and is connected to the equipment used to evaluate its performance. The photographer, John Click, worked as a technical assistant at the test centre.

Click RTS 87B

Great Western Railway broad gauge locomotives at Swindon Works
in 1892. The GWR finally abandoned the 7 ft 0¼ins broad gauge
system in May 1892 and to accommodate the redundant locomotives
and rolling stock withdrawn from service several miles of sidings
were laid at Swindon. Of the 195 locomotives taken out of service
130 were of the 'convertible' type which re-entered traffic as
standard gauge engines. This sort of mass gathering of locomotives
for scrapping was not seen again until the withdrawal of BR's steam
locomotive fleet in the 1960s.

GWR E2/62

The end of the line on the Little Eaton Gangway near Derby. This view of derelict wagons at Denby Colliery by the Midland Railway's photographer T. A. Scotton was one of a series recording the last operational parts of this horse-drawn plateway. It was taken on 29th September 1908, shortly before closure. The line was built to feed coal and other bulk traffic to the Derby Canal and used 'tram' or flanged rails and horses to pull its wagons.

Derby 8912

The remains of a Great Western Railway broad gauge carriage, slowly disintegrating in a Gloucestershire garden in 1967.

Pearce-Higgins 1967/B12

As steam declined on British Railways enthusiasts turned their attention to industrial locomotives, which had been largely neglected by railway photographers until the 1950s. National Coal Board locomotives 0-6-2T No.31, and 0-6-0ST No.63 were photographed in 1967 at the Lambton Railway's Philadelphia shed in County Durham.

Pearce-Higgins 1967/B6

Woodhams Scrapyard at Barry in Glamorgan was to have broken up over 200 locomotives, withdrawn from British Railways at the end of steam in the 1960s. However, they were not immediately scrapped and eventually nearly all of them were saved by preservation groups. The 2-6-2T locomotive No.4144, on the left, was rescued by the Great Western Society and restored to working order at Didcot, whilst the 0-6-0PT locomotive No.9681 was recovered to run on the Dean Forest Railway.

Pearce-Higgins 1974/2

Cyril Herbert chose an unconventional, but eyecatching, way of photographing the preserved Great Northern Railway 'Stirling Single' locomotive No.1 in 1947, producing this detailed view through the driver's window.

Herbert R13 C2 21